THE COMPLETE TOOLKIT FOR
BUSY WOMEN WITH ADHD

Manage Your Time, Regulate Your
Emotions & Organise Your Life
In Just **10 Minutes A Day**

Copyright © 2024 by LearnWell Books.

All rights reserved. No part of this publication may be reproduced, distributed, or transmitted in any form or by any means, including photocopying, recording, or other electronic or mechanical methods, without the prior written permission of the publisher, except in the case of brief quotations embodied in critical reviews and certain other noncommercial uses permitted by copyright law.

References to historical events, real people, or real places are often fictitious. In such cases, the names, characters, and places are products of the author's imagination. We do this where it's important to protect the privacy of people, places, and things.

689 Burke Rd
Camberwell Victoria 3124
Australia

www.LearnWellBooks.com

We're led by God. Our business is also committed to supporting kids' charities. At the time of printing, we have donated well over $100,000 to enable mentoring services for underprivileged children. By choosing our books, you are helping children who desperately need it. Thank you.

This Is Really Important.
It's a Sincere Thank You.

My name is Wayne, the founder of LearnWell.

My Dad put a book in my hands when I was 13. It was written by Zig Ziglar and it changed the course of my life. Since then, it's been books that have helped me get over breakups, learn how to be a good friend, study the lives of good people and books have been the source of my persistence through some pretty challenging times.

My purpose is now to return the favor. To create books that might be the turning point in the lives of people around the world, just like they've been for me. It's enough to almost bring me to tears to think of you holding this book, seeking information and wisdom from something that I've helped to create. I'm moved in a way that I can't fully explain.

We're a small and 'beyond-enthusiastic' team here at LearnWell. We're writers, editors, researchers, designers, formatters (oh ... and a bookkeeper!) who take your decision to learn with us incredibly seriously. We consider it a privilege to be part of your learning journey. Thank you for allowing us to join you.

If there's anything we did really well, anything we messed up, or anything AT ALL that we could do better, would you please write to us and tell us (like, right now!) We would love to hear from you!

readers@learnwellbooks.com

We're sending you our thanks, our love and our very best wishes.

Wayne
and the team at LearnWell Books.

WELCOME TO OUR COMMUNITY

"It's like a private online book club"

 Imagine if you could actually meet and talk with other readers of this book and share your experiences.

 Imagine if you could chat with the author or join them on a live Q&A!

 Imagine getting access to the author's notes and other exclusive, unpublished material.

You can do all of that and a lot more in the LearnWell Online Community!!

→ Download your **Workbook**
→ Chat directly with the author!
→ Meet and feel supported by other readers and their experiences.
→ Access additional, exclusive content about this topic and others.
→ Join our live Author Q&A sessions online.
→ Learn faster, make lasting changes, and have 10 times more fun!

This is part of our commitment to creating the best learning resources in the world.

Scan the QR code to get FREE access
www.learnwellbooks.com/organized

To my female heroes

It may have felt as though you've been alone on this path.

You're not.

I hope you draw immense comfort from knowing that there is a league of strong, capable, accomplished women here with you.

We love you.

And we believe in your unlimited capacity.

CONTENTS

Introduction — 12

PART 1: UNDERSTANDING YOUR UNIQUE ADHD BRAIN — 17

1. Not Broken, Brilliant — 18
   Uncovering The Hidden Strengths Of Your ADHD Mind

2. The Female ADHD Experience — 25
   Navigating Hormones, Life Stages, And Symptoms

3. ADHD Truths Unveiled — 34
   Debunking Myths And Embracing Reality

PART 2: MASTERING YOUR EMOTIONS — 41

4. Emotional Intelligence For ADHD — 42
   From Overwhelm To Control

5. The Plan For Peace — 50
   Building Daily Stability

6. Self-Compassion As A Superpower — 56
   Nurturing Your ADHD Self

7	The ADHD Journal Revolution	62
	Clarity In Five Minutes A Day	
8	Therapy Techniques Tailored For You	69
	CBT And DBT Strategies For ADHD Minds	
9	Be Your Own Therapist	77
	Customizing CBT And DBT Techniques For Your Unique Experience	
10	The Mood Reset Button	87
	5 Quick Emotional Regulation Techniques	
11	Mindfulness For The Active Mind	97
	Practical Methods For ADHD Brains	

PART 3: OPTIMIZING DAILY LIFE — 105

12	Time Mastery For ADHD	106
	Strategies For Productivity And Punctuality	
13	From Chaos To Order	112
	Simple Organization Techniques	
14	Creating Helpful Habits	118
	How To Build Routines That Stick	
15	Procrastination To Action	126
	Motivation Techniques That Work	
16	Focused And Flourishing	133
	Harnessing Concentration On Demand	

PART 4: THRIVING IN LIFE AND RELATIONSHIPS — 141

17 Optimizing Your Wellness — 142
Holistic Approaches To ADHD Health

18 Building Your Social Circle — 149
Friendship Strategies For Women With ADHD

19 Love And ADHD — 157
Nurturing Healthy Partnerships

20 The Impulse Advantage — 168
Channeling ADHD Energy Positively

21 Goal Setting for the ADHD Mind — 175
Turning Aspirations Into Achievements

PART 5: PROFESSIONAL LIFE, SUPERHUMAN SKILLS & THE IMPORTANCE OF SUPPORT — 183

22 Your Quirks At Work Are Your Trademark — 184
Standing Out In A Sea Of Sameness

23 Leading With Empathy — 192
Your ADHD Advantage In Communication

24 Finding Your Professional Niche — 200
Aligning Career With ADHD Strengths

25	Your ADHD Tribe	205
	Creating A Network That Elevates You	

Conclusion 211

References 213

YOUR WORKBOOK

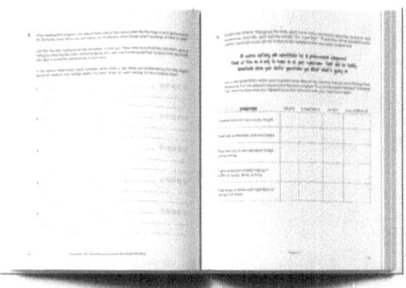

A shocking truth was discovered by a study done in 1987 – **people only remember 10% of what they read!**

That seems so discouraging.

But here's the **GOOD NEWS** – reading is **NEVER** a waste of time. As long as you do **one** important thing ...

The same study (by National Training Laboratories) shows that you will remember 90% of what you read when you **put your new knowledge into action**!

Here at LearnWell, we aim to create **the world's best learning resources**. So, we have included a highly engaging **Workbook** that helps you put your new knowledge into fun, practical action.

So, make sure you download your **FREE Workbook.** You'll find it located inside the **LearnWell Community.** Simply scan the QR code below for access.

Get your Workbook in the LearnWell Community
Scan the QR Code for access or go to:
www.learnwellbooks.com/organized

INTRODUCTION

According to the National Institute of Mental Health (NIMH), 13% of adult males will be diagnosed with ADHD at some point in their life. Just 4.2% of women will be diagnosed.[1]

In 2017, I became one of them.

When I was a child, not much was known about ADHD. What people did know was filled with stereotypes – and all aimed at boys. It was believed that only boys suffered from neurodevelopmental issues like ADHD and autism. Girls were lucky. They escaped having to deal with the impulsivity, the emotional outbursts, and constant getting into trouble because their ADHD had led them astray.

Only now it turns out that's not true.

All those stereotypes have long since been dismissed as it became recognized that girls and women do suffer from ADHD. We just behave differently.

I find it hard to describe how I felt when I got my diagnosis. There was relief that I wasn't crazy. This was my reality and not me making it up for attention. There was sadness about the childhood I could have had if I'd had the right support. I worried about what would happen now that I had a label that would follow me for life. I felt angry at all those times I got in trouble for things I couldn't help.

So. Many. Emotions.

Learning about ADHD became my new hyperfocus. I threw myself into researching the condition and why women have been looked over for so long. What could I do to make my life better? What could I do to overcome all the challenges I'd dealt with my whole life?

One thing soon became very clear: what works for so-called 'neurotypical' people rarely works for those of us whose brains are what I like to call 'neurospicy.' It didn't matter how much I wanted to get organized. I could buy all the journals and write all the to-do lists, but they flew out the window when it came to actually doing.

I discovered that women with ADHD have problems with what's called 'executive functioning.' More on that later, but for now, let's just say no wonder I had problems with organization! If something was out of sight, I plain forgot about it. I was like a baby playing peekaboo. If it was hidden, it didn't exist. Keeping important things locked up in filing cabinets? The worst possible thing you could do to someone with ADHD!

I'd go through phases of overwhelm. I had so much to do I didn't know where to start. Then I'd hit the other end of the extreme where I'd do all the things. Or rather, I'd start trying to do all of them. I'd flit from one task to the next. I'd get a bit done, but then I'd get distracted before I finished. My brain felt like a hummingbird on speed. I couldn't keep up with my thoughts.

My whole life, I'd just muddled through. But now I had the key to my problems: ADHD. Having an explanation for my issues meant that there had to be a solution. I was going to find it.

The book you hold in your hands is the result of years of work and experimentation. As a woman with ADHD, I've faced so much frustration. I've dealt with trying and failing to be 'normal', whatever that means. Women have been overlooked for so long. It's only relatively recently that research has shown how our ADHD manifests differently to men's. Now I know the signs, it's obvious that I have ADHD – and always have.

There's nothing quite like people with an ADHD brain. We're highly creative. It's no surprise that so many famous people are starting to open up about their ADHD. Justin Timberlake, will.i.am, Howie Mandell, Paris Hilton, Emma Watson... The list goes on. While they all talk about how hard ADHD makes life, it's also true that they wouldn't be who they are without it.

That's not all. We're filled with energy. We can focus on something for hours, long after anyone else would give up. We're resilient. Whatever life throws at us, we'll just throw it right back! We're spontaneous. No one's more fun than someone with ADHD.

I've designed this book with busy women in mind. The chapters are short. They cover the main issues facing women with ADHD. I get straight to the point – no waffle, just simple, practical advice that has worked for me and the women with whom I've shared this information.

You don't have to read the chapters in order, either. You can go straight to what's most important to you. I've made sure you've got everything you need to overcome your ADHD challenges. If you want to turn to the chapter that interests you most, go for it. Whatever works for you. By the end, you'll have learned how to reach your full potential as a bundle of ADHD awesomeness!

Plus, I've created a brilliant Workbook that will allow you to implement all of these tools in 10-minute blocks each day. You'll see more information about that on the following pages but I want to strongly encourage you to get your copy of this. Reading is powerful but when you take action, the ideas from a book can truly make a difference in your life.

With me as your guide, you'll learn how to understand ADHD and its unique impact on women. We'll explore emotional regulation so you're not at the mercy of your emotions anymore. We'll go through some of the basics of self-help with proven strategies that support ADHD. Together, we'll figure out how you can best navigate your life.

Get organized? You'll find out how easy it is. Establish routines? You'll see how helpful they are – when they're done right. Find support? The LearnWell Community's got your back. As for procrastination, we'll finally get around to tackling that!

By the end of this book, you'll have joined the thousands of busy women I've helped and you'll see ADHD for what it really is – a strength, not a burden. Not only will you understand ADHD so much more – you'll also understand and appreciate yourself.

With my love and support,
Alethea

PART 1

Understanding Your Unique ADHD Brain

NOT BROKEN, BRILLIANT

Uncovering The Hidden Strengths Of Your ADHD Mind

"You may not have ADHD! You may just be a restless, impatient, anxious, driven, mercurial, moody, forgetful, distracted, motor-mouthing, mind-wandering space cadet who never finishes anything, can't do paperwork, doesn't listen, and self-medicates with caffeine, cannabis, and cigarettes."

– Ava Green

I jolt awake, panicked that I've missed my meeting. Scrabbling for my phone, I relax when I see it's only 7am. I roll over and am instantly asleep again. When my alarm goes off, I instinctively hit the snooze button. And again. And again. When it eventually registers that maybe I should be getting up, I really do panic. My meeting is at 10. I've got a whopping ten minutes to get ready.

I go to fetch the outfit I wanted to wear. It's not in my closet, so I check the dryer. I finally find the clothes I want in the washer. Wet.

I put the washer on again and find something vaguely acceptable in my hamper. It doesn't smell (much). I figure I can get one more day out of it.

I grab a breakfast bar to eat on the go and hurry out. I turn right back around and go inside again. I forgot my phone. It reckons I've got enough time to make my meeting if I hustle.

It's wrong. Between needing to fuel the car and trying – and failing – to avoid the speed cameras, I'm late.

I burst into my meeting, disrupting my co-workers, who were already deep into planning.

"I'm sorry I'm late. Traffic was-"

Before I could explain, my boss cut me off. "Everyone else managed to be here."

I hear what he doesn't say: I'm a total failure.

This is what life is like for so many women with ADHD. It was my daily experience until I learned how to work with my brain wiring.

SO WHAT IS ADHD ANYWAY?

ADHD stands for 'attention deficit hyperactivity disorder.' It used to be believed that it was a condition that only affected boys, who would eventually grow out of it. We now know that it's a lifelong neurological condition that affects both sexes. Put simply, those with ADHD have different neural wirings in their brain[1].

While official statistics show that there are almost twice as many males with ADHD than females, it's possible this is due to a lack of diagnosis. Males are more likely to be referred for a diagnosis than females. It's only natural more of them receive a diagnosis. What's more, women are often misdiagnosed with other conditions such as bipolar disorder or depression. Sadly, many professionals still don't understand that ADHD looks different in females. [2]

You've likely heard of a related condition: autism. You may have heard the saying that if you've met one person with autism, you've met one person with autism. This is because it's a spectrum and displays differently in individuals.

But did you know the same is true of ADHD?

While there is a list of symptoms associated with ADHD, you probably don't have all of them. And those that you do exhibit will manifest differently in each individual.

THE THREE VARIETIES OF ADHD

There are three different types of ADHD:

- **ADHD, Hyperactive-impulsive type.** More common in males than females, those with this type will tend towards hyperactivity and impulsivity. Behavior tends to be externalized. It can include being disruptive and aggressive. It can even result in self-destructive tendencies such as substance abuse or misspending.

- **ADHD, Inattentive type.** More common in females than males, this is often overlooked because issues are internalized. As such, others may not notice you're struggling. You can be easily distracted. You may have been told off for daydreaming when you were at school. Maybe you still are during boring meetings.

- **ADHD, Combined type.** As you'd expect, those with this type exhibit a combination of behaviors from both types.

Since girls are typically more compliant in school, their struggles are overlooked. We weren't causing trouble for the teachers. Boys with ADHD got more attention because they were interrupting the class.

Going into adulthood, undiagnosed ADHD in women can manifest in numerous ways. These are some of the most common:

- Daydreaming or your mind wandering
- Anxiety (which can lead to being diagnosed with an anxiety disorder rather than the actual cause)

- Depression
- Zoning out while talking
- Getting easily distracted
- Problems with processing sound and language
- Forgetfulness
- Disordered eating or eating disorders
- Hypersexuality
- Problems with staying calm and patient
- Stimming (Repetitive movements such as fidgeting, pulling hair, etc.)
- Easily fatigued
- Problems sleeping
- Feeling overwhelmed by your emotions, perhaps even crying
- Struggling in social situations
- Perfectionism
- Poor body image
- People-pleasing
- Feeling that you're not living up to your potential
- Poor self-esteem

THE IMPACT OF LATE DIAGNOSIS

*I wasn't diagnosed with ADHD until I was 37. While it was a relief to have an explanation for why I'd always struggled at school, there was so much to figure out. Who was I really? Was I lazy or was it ADHD? How much of my behaviors were part of me, and how much was developed to cope with my ADHD? I felt like I had more questions than answers.
– Rebecca H.*

If you're not diagnosed until later in life, like I was, you've got even more to deal with. I've spent years learning how my ADHD has affected me. The older you get, the more complicated things become. Is it ADHD, or is it trauma? Bipolar disorder? Anxiety? Depression? All of the above??

It is important to remember that ADHD is hardwired into you from birth. While it might not always be obvious, if you have ADHD, it's always affected you. You won't lose it. You might learn coping mechanisms. It might look different as you age. But you won't get rid of it.

This is why it's so hard to get a diagnosis when you're older. Think back to when you were a child. Were you daydreaming in class all the time? Did you struggle to focus? Were you dismissed as lazy, even though you knew you were working really hard? Did you wish you found it easy to get organized like your classmates?

When you're diagnosed, you'll be asked to talk about what you were like as a child. Ideally, your clinician will ask your family members as well. They may have noticed things you didn't realize you were doing because of your ADHD. You may have grown out of those behaviors, but you haven't grown out of your ADHD.

Left untreated, you may have found that things have intensified as you aged. You may even have only recently suspected you have ADHD.[3] As we learn more about ADHD and how it manifests in women, awareness is slowly increasing. This is a positive thing. The more we know about ADHD, the more we can learn about ourselves if you're someone with the condition.

Since it's important to be aware that ADHD presents differently in women, we'll explore this more deeply in the next chapter. Read on to learn more about why so many women are misdiagnosed. We'll also explore how fluctuating hormones and a woman's different life stages affect ADHD symptoms.

THE FEMALE ADHD EXPERIENCE

Navigating Hormones, Life Stages, And Symptoms

"Despite the absence of gender differences in ADHD, girls tend to be diagnosed later in their lives even though they may have more functional impairments"

– Ellen B. Littman, PhD

> *ADHD? Doesn't that only affect boys?*

> *You just need to go for a run. Get some exercise, and you'll be fine!*

> *ADHD was invented to sell drugs. It's Big Pharma trying to make more money. It doesn't exist.*

I could have played ADHD Bingo with all the phrases that were repeated at me. Even with a diagnosis, people didn't always take this condition seriously. The stereotype of ADHD being a disability that only affects boys persists. I even had someone tell me that ADHD was created to medicate boys to stop being boys. Boys like roughhousing! Boys have more energy! They need to work off that steam. Of course, they're going to play up if they don't get to run around.

LIVING UP TO SOCIETY'S EXPECTATIONS (AND FAILING)

The reality is that ADHD most likely affects both genders equally. However, it manifests differently in women because of societal and cultural expectations. We get dismissed as being "too much." We do our best to tone ourselves down, but we can't always control those impulses caused by ADHD.

Our ADHD means it's harder to make friends. We tend to be social creatures. Feeling like we can't get the support we need from other women compounds the issue. It doesn't help that we struggle to meet social expectations of us. We find it hard to be on time. We forget social commitments, even when it's something we really want to do. We struggle not to interrupt, but if we don't, we'll forget what we were going to say. Keeping a lid on things others might find rude or inappropriate is exhausting. And we want to follow conversations, we really do, but it's so easy to get distracted. Then people think we don't care about what they're saying, and it's not true.

We simply can't help it.[1]

For many of us, this has been our life for as long as we can remember. ADHD women don't match societal expectations. Our impulsiveness, emotional ups and downs, messiness, lack of attention to grooming, and disorganization counter what we're "supposed" to be like. Times might be changing, but women are still expected to conform in a way that's virtually impossible for ADHD women. When you're young, boys can get away with it because they're, well, boys! But girls get constant criticism because we're not fitting into the girly box. We're supposed to be better organized, better presented, and just plain nicer. We learn from an early age that we're not good enough. It doesn't matter how hard we try. We never will be.[2]

It was a real lightbulb moment for me to understand that this is how I'm wired. I am who I am and if that's not good enough for society, tough! I can't change, and it's about time that was accepted.

WOMEN GET MISDIAGNOSED MORE THAN MEN. FACT.

I knew something was wrong, but I didn't know what. When I went to the doctor for help, I was diagnosed with bipolar disorder. It took years before a recently diagnosed friend told me she thought I had ADHD, too. With her help, I found a supportive doctor. He diagnosed me with ADHD. Finally, I had the answer to my problems. The medication I'd been given for bipolar disorder had never really worked for me. Now I knew why. – Alice M.

It's these gender expectations that have a lot to do with the underdiagnosis and misdiagnosis of girls who grow up to be underdiagnosed or misdiagnosed women. We're less of a problem to society. We're less disruptive. What's more, historically, women get dismissed as being hysterical or exaggerating. One study showed that women's pain was more likely to be underestimated and underreported. We get sent for psychotherapy when what we need is what men get – pain relief![3]

This gender bias persists. Research has shown that males get referred for help because of issues with behavior. Females were more likely to be referred because of emotional problems like anxiety or depression[4]. It isn't always questioned whether ADHD could cause those emotional problems. Instead, those become the focus. Girls and women are often given non-ADHD medications such as antidepressants. It can take years before the real cause is unearthed. We're glossed over by parents and teachers. Our problems are dismissed until we're suffering much more. Meanwhile, boys are referred for diagnosis and treatment far sooner.

THE IMPACT OF LIFE STAGES ON ADHD

In addition to social influences, hormones are believed to affect how ADHD impacts women. Estrogen, the main sex hormone in females, is mainly associated with reproduction. However, it is also connected with cognitive functions. It affects dopamine, serotonin, and norepinephrine, which are all neurotransmitters that affect mood, focus, and memory.

While estrogen isn't a miracle cure for ADHD and isn't its underlying cause, it most definitely affects us. When estrogen is high, our cognitive and executive functions work better than when it's low. Given that our estrogen levels are always changing, it's no wonder we have good and bad days. [5]

Puberty

   They say that puberty is hell, but it was way worse than that for me. I was all over the place. People would ask, "What's wrong with you?" I didn't have a clue! – Tamsin T.

Puberty usually affects girls between 9-13. It brings with it a range of physical and emotional changes. We're becoming women. Estrogen and progesterone levels increase. While more estrogen might make things better for girls with ADHD, progesterone doesn't. Things often get worse.[6]

If you've been fortunate enough to get a diagnosis, ADHD medications often don't work as well. You might find it helpful to track your symptoms so you can talk about them with your doctor.

Menstruation

My poor husband knows that for half the month I'm going to be a nightmare to live with. Over the years, I've learned what helps. Going for a swim to get some exercise is good. It's also a great excuse to sit in the hot tub! I watch my diet and avoid foods that make me feel worse, like pizza and fries. Still, I always dread PMS. – Karly S.

Most women menstruate monthly. It starts at puberty and goes until perimenopause. You could have periods for around 40 years. This means you've got decades of fluctuating hormone levels. If your ADHD is going haywire, chances are it has to do with your estrogen and progesterone being all over the place. The last two weeks of your cycle are said to be the worst. This is because progesterone levels are high.[7] It's also been suggested that we suffer more from premenstrual syndrome (PMS). Yay.[8]

Be kind to yourself. You're not going mad. You've got ADHD! Track your cycles and see if you notice what makes things worse. You might find certain foods are a trigger, particularly processed things. Yep, all that comfort food might not really be a comfort. Some women find exercise helps. The most important thing is to understand that we all have bad days. Don't be so hard on yourself because some days are a struggle.

Pregnancy

> *I wish I could have enjoyed my pregnancy more. We'd been trying for a baby for ages. I'd had dreams of decorating the nursery and buying baby clothes. But instead, I found myself becoming a blubbering mess. My emotions were all over the place. I couldn't get organized. Trying to plan anything was a nightmare. My ADHD took over and I hated it.*
> *– Rae N.*

If you fall pregnant, you're also subject to major changes in your hormones. This means that you could find yourself suffering more from your ADHD symptoms in the first trimester. You may experience this before you realize you're pregnant, which can make things tough. Or you may have stopped taking your ADHD medication because of your pregnancy. This makes the first trimester a time of adjustment on so many levels. Not only is your body changing to support your baby, but you're also adapting to becoming a mother. On top of all that, you're figuring out how to function without your meds if you decide to stop.[7]

Be aware that it may not be necessary to stop taking your medication. It's worth talking to your doctor about any concerns. You may be able to lower the dose or keep taking them as you always have.

Menopause

> *When I hit the menopause, I had mixed emotions. Part of me was glad that the nightmare of my*

> *periods was finally ending. But I had other issues to deal with now. I had major brain fog and found it even harder to concentrate. It felt like if it wasn't one thing, it was another. – Sharon C.*

Perimenopause often kicks in around 40. Estrogen starts to go down, and menstruation becomes less regular. This stage can last as long as ten years before a woman enters menopause and stops menstruating completely.

While some women have little issue with menopause, for others, it can be debilitating. Just when you thought mood swings were over, you can find them back with a vengeance due to the changes in hormone levels. Menopause can also result in hot flushes, memory issues, and trouble focusing. If you have ADHD, you may already find it hard to focus. This only compounds the issue.[9]

A discussion with your doctor is a necessary step if you feel that menopause is making things worse for you. There are various treatments available, such as Hormone Replacement Therapy (HRT). These can alleviate the symptoms of menopause, helping you with your ADHD.

The one constant in life is change. Just when you think you've figured out how to deal with your ADHD, something else comes along to throw you a curveball. The various stages of the female cycle require different approaches. What I found helpful was to keep track of my symptoms. There are lots of apps you can use if you don't want to write things down. I use the health app that came with my phone. After a while, I started to notice patterns that made it easier for me to talk about things with my doctor.

One of the biggest lessons I've had to learn as a woman with ADHD is that you are your best advocate. Sadly, our issues aren't always taken seriously. Don't be afraid to switch medics until you find a doctor who listens and understands what you're going through. Make a list of what you need to discuss so you don't forget any symptoms. Let them know what's worked for you and what hasn't. We've prepared a template of such a list in your Workbook for you to fill in, which will make your next doctor's visit a breeze. No more mental scrambling as you try to recall your concerns!

Communication is a two-way street. You'll get the most out of your healthcare providers when you can tell them exactly what's going on. They can then go through the various options so you can work together to find the best solution.

A persistent issue is that there's been so much misinformation about ADHD in women. While things are improving, there are still pervading myths that some people—including medics—buy into. That's why we will explore these in the next chapter. Giving people more accurate information becomes easier when you know why and how they're mistaken. Even if it can be a little disheartening that people can think like that in this day and age…

3

ADHD TRUTHS UNVEILED

Debunking Myths And Embracing Reality

"Society's answer to an increase in ADHD diagnoses shouldn't be, "Oh my God, everyone has ADHD now." It should be, "Oh my God, how did we manage to let so many people down?"

– Ellie Middleton

Remember when I mentioned ADHD Bingo? It's when you take all the phrases people throw at you, and every time someone says one of them, you cross it off your list. The first one to cross them all out wins.

If I ever played, I won every time. I don't know what was worse. Well-meaning strangers trying to make me feel better because "we all have ADHD really"? Family members telling me it's all in my head? None of them saw the hours I spent researching my condition. None of them were inside my brain, seeing how hard it was for me to do what they took for granted.

Despite the name, ADHD Bingo isn't fun.

I could have written a whole book based on ADHD Bingo phrases. Instead, I'm just going to give you a chapter.

MYTH #1 – ADHD ISN'T REAL

Science has proven it. People with ADHD have a different brain makeup than those without. There are chemical differences between neurotypical and neurodiverse people. Brain imaging scans demonstrate that our brains are actually wired differently. It's fascinating stuff. It's also proof positive that while ADHD might be in our minds, that doesn't make it fake. It's a very real condition.[1]

MYTH #2 – PEOPLE WITH ADHD CAN NEVER FOCUS

This one dates back to when people first started learning about ADHD. It's all in the name – Attention Deficit Hyperactivity

Disorder. The truth is that if you have ADHD, it's not that you can't focus. You have lots of attention, not a deficit of it. If anything, you may be highly sensitive to the world around you. You may notice things other people don't. What you struggle with is controlling where your focus goes. That's why those of us with ADHD are so easily distracted. We start discussing one thing, then... SQUIRREL![2]

MYTH #3 – IF YOU HAVE ADHD, YOU'RE JUST NOT TRYING HARD ENOUGH

Speaking from personal experience, years of trying harder made no difference. We don't tell someone with a broken leg they just need to try harder to walk. Why should it be any different for someone with ADHD? A short-sighted person can't see better with more effort. Someone with ADHD can't change their brain's wiring just because they want to. There are strategies you can put in place to make things easier for yourself. We'll go into those later. But hard work and wishful thinking won't cut it.

MYTH #4 – YOU CAN GET OVER ADHD IF YOU'RE SMART

The opposite is true. People with higher IQs are less likely to get help and support. This is because they often figure out ways of masking their symptoms. They manage to get by in school by finding ways to compensate for their procrastination, problems focusing, and other issues. If they're excited by a certain subject, they can excel and pursue fulfilling careers. None of that makes their ADHD go away, though. They still struggle. They just may end up coping alone and suffer more than they should.[3]

MYTH #5 – THERE ARE MEDICATIONS TO CURE ADHD

There is no cure for ADHD. Medication can alleviate the symptoms, though. Studies show that medications help roughly 80% of the time[4]. It's like wearing glasses. They won't stop you from being long—or short-sighted. While you're wearing them, you can see clearly. Take them off, and the world goes fuzzy again. It's the same with medication. You have to keep taking it to get the benefit. Stop, and you're right back where you started.

MYTH #6 – ADHD ONLY AFFECTS KIDS

ADHD is a lifelong condition. You don't grow out of it. It's with you forever. This is why so many overlooked kids don't get diagnosed until later. While you may not be diagnosed until adulthood, you will have had those traits since childhood.

MYTH #7 – ADHD IS CAUSED BY SOCIAL MEDIA

There's no doubt we live in a world of information overload. Doom-scrolling your way through reels and videos is an easy way to lose a few hours. We've got stimuli thrown at us all the time. While it may be having an effect on people's ability to focus for longer, it's not the same as developing ADHD. You can't get it as an adult, and you certainly can't catch it from social media.

MYTH #8 – IF YOU'VE GOT ADHD, YOU'RE HYPERACTIVE (AND YOU MUST BE MALE)

People know about the hyperactive aspect of ADHD because it's the most visible. You can see when someone's struggling to stay still or finding it hard to control their urges. But there's so much more to ADHD than being hyperactive. This is where gender plays a major part. Girls and women with ADHD are less likely to deal with hyperactivity but still have to cope with issues with executive function and inattentiveness. They tend to deal more with depression and anxiety[5]. It's made worse because we're less likely to be diagnosed. People don't believe we can have ADHD, so we're struggling through it on our own.

MYTH #9 – ADHD ISN'T A BIG DEAL

All the myths we've already gone through probably explain why people think ADHD isn't a big deal. We just need medication! We're women! We don't suffer from it anyway! Thinking ADHD isn't that serious isn't just wrong. It's potentially dangerous. A study by the National Institutes of Health showed that people with ADHD were more likely to get involved in self-destructive behaviors such as:

- Substance abuse
- Eating disorders/Disordered eating
- Risky sexual behavior
- Impulsivity

What's more, women with ADHD were 6x more likely to put themselves at risk[6]. Since these types of behavior can have serious consequences, the impact of ADHD should not be underestimated.

Only 20% of adults with ADHD know they have ADHD!

MYTH #10 – EVERYBODY KNOWS ABOUT ADHD. WE DON'T NEED ANY MORE AWARENESS

ADHD may be featured more in the media these days. That doesn't mean people are better informed about it. The myths in this chapter alone show that's not true. And that's just the tip of the iceberg. In fact, ADHD understanding is still woefully low, especially when it comes to adult women with ADHD. Research suggests that only 20% of adults with ADHD know they have ADHD. That means that 80% of people with ADHD are walking around, unaware that the reason why they're struggling is because they have ADHD. Until that statistic changes, we most definitely need more awareness[7].

Now that we've explored the impact of ADHD, it's time to get real. We will dive deep into practical strategies to help you work with your ADHD. It doesn't have to be a battle. ADHD can be positive – *if* you learn how to work with it instead of fighting against it.

And it all starts with learning how to regulate your emotions more effectively.

PART 2

Mastering Your Emotions

4

EMOTIONAL INTELLIGENCE FOR ADHD

From Overwhelm To Control

"You do control the thoughts that follow an emotion, and how you have a great deal of say in how you react to an emotion – as long as you are aware of it."

– Travis Bradberry

It was actually my mom who made me realize I probably had ADHD. Not because she kept telling me she thought I had it, but because she got diagnosed herself, and I saw the difference it made. Once she started on the treatment plan her clinicians put together for her, it was like she was a totally different person, and she was all the better for it. When I asked her about it, she said things were so different because she didn't get distracted anymore. If she was in the middle of something and an email or text came in, she was able to leave it until she was finished. In the past, she would have to stop everything to deal with it and nothing got done.

What was even more amazing was that my mom had always been a really emotional person. It was like she felt everything sooo deeply, and I was just like her. I never understood why other people didn't cry as much as I did or have these over-the-top reactions to a funny movie. Working with her therapist, she'd been able to get those reactions under control.

Seeing her go through this amazing transformation made me wonder whether I could do the same. I'd been struggling with so many of the problems she had. That's what gave me the push to get a diagnosis, and I'm so glad I did. – Gail L.

Understanding of ADHD is spreading. Most people understand that ADHD causes issues with focus and impulsivity. But what most people don't hear about as much is the problems we have with dealing with our emotions.

It's not that we have different emotions. Happiness is happiness. Sadness is sadness. What's different with ADHD is that we can feel these emotions in a much more intense way. They're overwhelming. Our emotions often linger for longer. They can stop us from doing things we need because we're having to figure out how to cope with our emotions.

As a result, women with ADHD can:

- Find themselves feeling discouraged, frustrated, or angry and do not understand why they're feeling so strongly
- Give up too soon on things they need to do
- Avoid dealing with other people[1]

While managing one's emotions can become easier with age, many people still struggle with emotional regulation throughout their lives.

> *I always felt sorry for my friends. If I was finding it difficult to manage my emotions, how hard was it for them having to put up with me having yet another meltdown? I thought it wasn't fair for them to have to deal with me, so I ended up pushing people away. – Camilla B.*

BREATHING EXERCISES

When we're stressed, our bodies naturally respond with shallow breathing in the upper chest. If we consciously change our breathing to use the diaphragm more, we can help calm our nervous system. This helps the body to relax, which has a knock-on effect on our emotional regulation as a whole. [2] And the great thing about using the breath to control your emotions is it's free! You can do it any time, any place for immediate relief. Nobody needs to know what you're doing so you don't feel like you stand out as "weird."

Here are some exercises you can try:

Counting The Breath

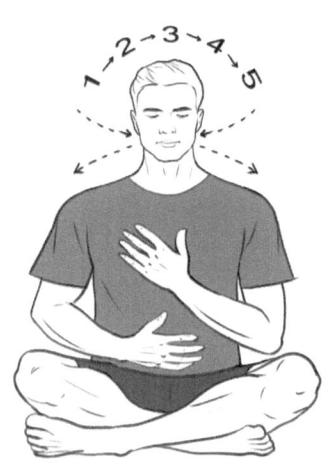

Breathe in for a count of 4.

Hold your breath for a count of 4.

Exhale for a count of 6.

Repeat as much as needed until you feel calm.

Breathing With The Diaphragm

Focus on your breath. Consciously take it all the way down to your stomach. Watch as your stomach rises as you inhale and lowers as you exhale. Follow this movement for at least ten cycles of breath.

If you find it hard to breathe into the diaphragm, you might find it easier to do this while lying down. Place one hand on your stomach and the other on your chest. Try to make only the hand on your stomach move, keeping the other still. Even if you find it difficult to start with, do your best. Watch the movement while you do this, and allow your breath to lull you into relaxation.

Bringing Meditation Into The Breath

If you prefer, you can combine your breathing with a meditation mantra. Mantras are sounds, words, or phrases you repeat as you meditate. Choose something that will support your emotional regulation, such as "Calm." As you inhale, silently say in your mind, "Calm." As you exhale, silently say, "Calm." Repeat for at least two minutes.

VISUALIZATION TECHNIQUES

Not everyone enjoys breathing exercises.
Some people find that their ADHD mind can't stop thinking about things. They don't slow down enough to be able to think solely about the breath.

If that's you, you might find that visualization works better for you. It gives the mind something to think about while visualizing something that helps you self-soothe. A beautiful visualization can help you get on top of those challenging emotions, leaving you feeling relaxed and at peace.

Safe Space Visualization

Creating a mental safe space gives you somewhere to go whenever you need a break from stress. The technique is simple:

Go somewhere you won't be disturbed and make yourself comfortable.

Close your eyes and take a few breaths to ground yourself in the moment. Allow yourself to relax with every exhale.

Now, picture in your mind's eye somewhere that makes you feel relaxed and safe. It might be somewhere you know, like your childhood home or a place in your garden with beautiful views. You could invent somewhere for your safe space, like a beach or under a tree by a stream.

Wherever you choose for your safe space, create it down to the tiniest detail. What does it look like? What can you hear? What does it smell like? What can you touch from where you're sitting?

Feel your breathing naturally slow and relax as you engage all your senses in creating a vivid, realistic experience in your mind. Know that you are completely safe here in this moment. If you find your mind drifting to other thoughts, gently bring it back to your safe space.

When you're ready to return to reality, gently let your visualization dissipate. Bring your awareness back to the room you're in. Gently stretch. Wiggle your fingers and toes. You might like to yawn.

When you're ready, open your eyes.

This safe space is yours. You can come anytime you need it, and no one can go there without your permission. Return whenever you need some moments of peace.

Meditating On A Candle Flame

Another way of visualizing is to imagine something in your mind to take your focus away from things that are upsetting you. With this technique, you might like to imagine a candle flame in your mind's eye. If you find this difficult, you could light a candle and place it in front of you, watching the flame until you're ready to close your eyes and recreate the flame in your mind.

Picture the center of the candle flame. Notice the colors you can see, maybe blues, whites, greens, reds, and oranges. 'See' the flame flicker, changing its shape as it burns. Notice how its glow can get lighter and dimmer. Watch how it never stays exactly the same. Allow yourself to be fascinated by the flame.

Let this simple visualization be the focus of your attention for as long as you need. When you're ready, allow the image of the flame to gently dissipate. Now, go about the rest of your day feeling calm and relaxed.

In your Workbook, you will have the opportunity to practice a quick 10-minute relaxation routine I have created for you. It's something you can use when you feel overwhelmed or simply as a practice to help you wind down at the end of your day. Try it out and consider practicing it daily!

In the next chapter, we'll examine ways of structuring your day to help you control your emotions.

5

THE PLAN FOR PEACE

Building Daily Stability

"Think of your emotions like little kids in the playground. They were given to you to care for, understand, and hold. Not to control, judge, or suppress. This awareness makes all the difference."

– Therapist_In_NYC

> *Do you find it hard to get started on tasks? And when you do, do you find it hard to keep going if it's not holding your interest?*

> *Absolutely!*

My therapist nodded and made a few notes. "There are a few strategies we can try that might help. Have you considered a daily checklist?"

The first time my therapist suggested it, I recoiled at the idea. Daily routines? No, thank you! Checklists? You need to be organized for those. How could I even put one together?

As we continued to explore the impact ADHD had on me, I started to change my mind. You see, most people with ADHD who aren't getting treatment find themselves gravitating towards activities that give them instant gratification. We love that immediate buzz of a reward! But tasks that aren't going to pay off for a while? It's so much harder. It's a risk. Emotionally, we don't know what the payoff is going to be. It's easier – and safer – to leave it for now. So, our to-do list grows and grows. We become more and more overwhelmed until we explode.

The ADHD stereotype focuses on our problems with focus or impulsivity. What's not talked about so much is the effect this has on our emotions. Emotional regulation occurs in the brain. When our working memory is overloaded because we're trying to do too much, our emotions take over. The brain becomes flooded with emotion. That's why we find ourselves suddenly feeling angry, frustrated or upset and out of control. It's like a computer virus taking up all a machine's computing capabilities. These emotions take over, and we physically can't do anything else.[1]

Our emotional highs and lows are so much higher and lower than someone without ADHD.[2] When those powerful emotions take charge, there's no space for thinking. We can't just put those feelings to one side. They're all we can think about.

MAKE THINGS EASY FOR YOUR BRAIN WITH A DAILY CHECKLIST

When my therapist explained it to me, it all made sense. However, I still didn't understand how that related to daily checklists. That was when she told me that these work because they make things easier for your brain. You don't have to remember everything you have to do. Trying to keep track of your to-do list in your head is more exhausting than you may realize.

A daily checklist allows you to block out the time available so you know what you need to do and when. Once you've set up your daily schedule, you can use the same outline every day and update it with the tasks for the day. You can then tick off tasks as you complete them. I find it incredibly satisfying to do this. It's that instant gratification buzz!

There are many templates and apps online that make it easy to create a checklist. Alternatively, you can find the one I use when I'm jotting things down on paper. I've shared more about this below, and I've included a copy in your Workbook.

Below, you will see some instructions for setting up your daily checklist:

1. Make a list of everything you have to do each day. Don't worry about putting them in order at this moment. Right now, you're just making sure you list everything you need to get done.

    Include your regular activities, such as your daily trip to the gym, regular meetings or appointments. You might like to get really detailed and include breaks and meals. This ensures you carve out time for lunch and don't forget to eat! I also include physical activity breaks. I find that if I'm struggling to make progress, I'm usually trying to do too much. Taking time out to go for a run or dance to some music gives my mind a break. When I return to work, I'm much more effective after some exercise. The rest of my list is full of one-off tasks. These could include making a phone call to book an appointment or working on an important project. Don't worry if you don't know everything you'll need to do. You can add things to your checklist as they arise.

2. Once you've made your list of tasks, you might feel overwhelmed by how big it is. Don't worry! This is where you start prioritizing. You won't always get everything done in a day, and that's okay. Getting the most important tasks out of the day will still give you a strong feeling of accomplishment.

    Sort items into high, medium, and low priority. If you find it hard to decide what's more urgent, don't hesitate to ask for help. If it's a work matter, ask your colleagues or manager to help you prioritize. If your list feels too long, consider whether you can delegate anything.

Once you've prioritized everything, you can start finalizing your checklist.

3. Assign a time frame to everything. Something might not seem important but needs to be completed within a certain time. I find it helpful to go through my list and assign the time I'll start the various tasks and how long each will take. I then use this to sort my schedule for the day. Of course, it doesn't have to be just work tasks, either. I include all the things I want to do for myself.

4. I can make a schedule for each day. My method is a little more advanced now compared to when I first started. I began with a pen and paper, as I'm suggesting for you. However, now that it's a habit for me, I've advanced to project management software to program everything in. That way, I don't have to keep remembering recurring tasks and can work around them. I use Asana, but there are lots of alternatives out there. I also like to write out my list for the day and put it up next to my computer monitor so I have a visual reminder. Crossing things off when I finish them is so rewarding. It gives me a dopamine rush of instant gratification! It works for bigger tasks, too. I break them down into smaller chunks so I can cross off each part. Seeing the progress I've made makes bigger tasks less overwhelming.

5. Let yourself be flexible. No matter how detailed your plans, things always come up. Think of your daily checklist as a guide rather than a rigid set of rules. You might not get everything you want done that day, but that's OK. Focus on

what you did get done. That's progress. Whatever you've achieved, you're closer to your goals as a consequence.

Turn to your Workbook to get a visual idea of how the Daily Checklist looks. This will add some context to my notes above, and the exercise there will show you how the Checklist works.

In addition to my Daily Checklist, I have a few sensory items on my desk. I have some stress balls and fidget spinners. I find it soothing to play with them while I'm putting together my checklist. They're also useful when I'm finding a task challenging or when I'm finding it hard to focus.

Although I find my daily checklist helpful, I still have times when I'm beating myself up for not being good enough. Things might be better than before my diagnosis, but it can be hard to stop comparing myself to other people. There are moments when I feel it's unfair that I have to work so hard when others have it so easy.

This is where practicing self-compassion comes in. In the next chapter, I'll walk you through some self-love exercises that will help you be compassionate with yourself on those days when things don't seem to be going well.

6

SELF-COMPASSION AS A SUPERPOWER

Nurturing Your ADHD Self

"You yourself, as much as anybody in the entire universe, deserve your love and affection."

– Buddha.

Ever watch "RuPaul's Drag Race?" I was hooked from the moment it first came onto our screens.

There was one thing RuPaul said that particularly resonated with me. He'd end episodes with, "If you can't love yourself, how the hell can you love anyone else? Can I get an Amen?" I'd join in with the cast chorusing *Amen!*

But the reality was that I didn't love myself, and I didn't see how anyone else could either, except maybe my mom. And that was only because she had to.

I was too much for one person to handle. Too emotional. Too impulsive. Too scatterbrained. It was only after my diagnosis that I understood why I was that way. But understanding didn't mean I liked myself more. It was only with the help of my therapist that I learned how to be kinder to myself. The more I gave myself love, the more I could forgive myself for those times when I was too much. And the more I forgave myself, the less I felt as though I was too much.

The work I did to love and accept myself changed everything. I was more confident and started saying yes to dates instead of thinking a relationship would be doomed to failure. But it was more than that. Being more comfortable with myself meant that I was also fine staying single. If I never met the man of my dreams, it would be okay. I could keep myself company and be happy.

When I met my boyfriend, Zach, romance was the last thing on my mind. I was too busy having fun, doing everything I'd never had the courage to do. I think it was the fact I *wasn't* looking for love that made it easy for him to come into my life. He's amazing. Our relationship is better than I could ever have imagined I deserved.

And it all came from loving myself first.

I'm going to take you through some of the exercises that worked for me. Some of them you can do when you need to, and others you might like to do every day—whatever makes you feel good! When you're kinder to yourself, you'll find you don't see your emotions as a problem anymore.

WATCH YOUR THOUGHTS

We all have an inner critic. This doesn't have to be a bad thing. Our inner critic helps us to improve. It asks us *could I do that differently*? It pushes us to do better. It supports us to be our best selves.

But sometimes, our inner critic pulls us down. It makes us think things that aren't true. That's why it's so important to watch our thoughts.

If you notice yourself putting yourself down, ask yourself whether you'd speak to a friend that way. You wouldn't, right? So why do it to yourself?

Reframe those thoughts. If you find yourself thinking something negative, think of a counter-argument.

Instead of thinking, "I'm always late," remind yourself that you're trying your best. You're implementing strategies to help you manage your time. You're improving, and you should congratulate yourself for that effort instead of beating yourself up.

REMIND YOURSELF HOW GREAT YOU ARE

If you're going through a rough patch, make a list of at least three things you like about yourself. If you're struggling to think of three things, consider the compliments people have paid you. It doesn't matter if the only things that come to mind are silly. They all count. You deserve to see how great you are. Let me guide you through a quick self-love practice in your Workbook.

Here are three things I like about myself:

1. My creativity. I see the world in a way no one else does. I love how it helps me to come up with out-of-the-box ideas.

2. My friends. I have the *best* people in my life! I figure that I can't be such a bad person if I can have friends as good as mine.

3. My freckles. I'm always being told how cute they are.

The more you start coming up with reasons to show yourself love, the more you see there is to love!

PRACTICE GRATITUDE

We'll explore journaling with gratitude in the next chapter, but I wanted to take a moment to discuss the importance of gratitude. Research shows that practicing gratitude has many mental and physical benefits. It can, for example, reduce anxiety and depression and improve overall well-being[1].

On top of my gratitude journal, I find it helpful to think of reasons to be grateful during the day. If my boss is being demanding, I say to myself that I'm grateful to have a job that gives me the chance to improve my communication. If I'm stuck in traffic, I remind myself I'm lucky to have a car, so I don't have to use public transport. If my ADHD symptoms are particularly bad, I tell myself that I'm grateful I have a diagnosis so I understand why I'm feeling that way. Whenever things are going wrong, I make a point of finding something to be grateful for about the situation. Now, I find it much easier to stay calm and focused.

I do this when I'm having a good time, too. When it's sunny and I'm at the beach, hanging out with friends, I smile and think about how grateful I am for this moment.

DO SOMETHING FOR YOURSELF EVERY DAY

It's so easy to get caught up in doing things for other people. I love helping others; it gives me a warm feeling inside.

But, as a busy woman, sometimes, you can spend the whole day doing everything everyone else needs and forget about what *you* need. Between work, friends, and family, it can feel like there's just not enough time in the day. So, how do we save time? By taking ourselves off our to-do list.

Prioritize yourself **first**. Schedule time in your Daily Checklist for something that makes you happy. It doesn't have to be much. It could just be a ten-minute meditation or yoga session. There are plenty of ten-minute workouts online. Getting your body moving can be a great pick-me-up. Alternatively, you could make yourself a hot drink and spend the time drinking it, thinking about things that make you happy.

Once you've gotten into the habit of spending ten minutes on yourself, you might find you want to take more time for yourself. That's okay! You deserve it! You could spend half an hour reading before you go to sleep, or you could go for a walk in nature.

Whatever it is, do at least one thing for yourself every single day.

In your Workbook, you'll find space to list everything you'd like to do for yourself. Once you've got your list, pick one thing and add it to your Daily Schedule tomorrow to make it happen. Promise yourself you will – and then keep your word! Whether you get up ten minutes earlier to do a short meditation or treat yourself to a nice pastry to have a quick break mid-afternoon, it'll help put a smile on your face and remind you that you *are* worth it.

One thing I do every day without fail is write in my journal. Journaling has made a massive difference to my emotional well-being. It's so important that I decided to devote an entire chapter to it. And that's what we're going to look at next!

7

THE ADHD JOURNAL REVOLUTION

Clarity In Five Minutes A Day

"Writing is medicine. It is an appropriate antidote to injury. It is an appropriate companion for any difficult change."

– Julia Cameron

"Boo-hoo! The baby's crying again!"

I'll never forget the jeering crowd gathered around me. There was one particular girl at elementary school who seemed to have it in for me. I was an easy target, I guess. Clumsy, forgetful, disorganized... There were so many things "wrong" with me.

The worst thing was that my emotions were an open book. It was easy to tell how I was feeling—you only had to look at my face. This made me ripe for bullying. I gave them the kind of reaction mean girls love.

Over time, I learned that emotions were something I was supposed to hide. But it didn't matter how hard I tried. I couldn't keep a lid on them. Being so emotional was another thing I couldn't control, unlike everyone else.

Still, I did my best. It made me lose touch with my emotions. I had no idea why I felt the way I did. I just knew that I felt *deeply*.

It was my therapist who suggested journaling as part of my therapy. At first, I resisted the idea. I graduated from school a long time ago. Who wants to start doing homework at my age? She reassured me it would only take 5-10 minutes a day and that I might find it helpful.

"Give it a try," she told me. "What have you got to lose?"

As it turned out, I had a *lot* of emotional baggage to lose, and journaling really helped me ditch it. Now, I journal at the start and end of every day and it's made such a difference to my emotional well-being. Understanding why I am the way I am has helped me feel more in control.

There are lots of different ways to journal, so I'm going to give you a couple of options to choose from. However you choose to do it, the basic principles will remain the same. They are:

- Choose somewhere you won't be disturbed while you journal.

- Write without censoring yourself. Your journal is for **you**. No one else gets to read it unless you want them to. This is the one place where you don't need to put any restrictions on yourself. The more you can let yourself be free and express yourself without fear, the more helpful you'll find it.

- Ideally, use pen and paper for your journal. While you can type it or dictate it into your phone, there's something about handwriting that enables you to explore further and feel into the process.

- Journal every day. Build it into your routine. I recommend adding it as a task on your daily checklist to ensure it gets done. As you journal more, you'll start to notice the benefits and look forward to it—like I do!

JOURNALING ABOUT YOUR FEELINGS

This journaling method was inspired by Nonviolent Communication, one way of improving how you communicate with others[1]. If you feel that you're out of touch with your emotions, this is a powerful way of rebuilding that link.

1. Think about a time that brought up strong emotions for you, either good or bad.

2. Relive this situation in your mind. Allow yourself to feel whatever emotions come up. If you're working with a difficult memory, you may experience painful emotions. Don't try to repress them. Sit with that feeling and allow yourself to fully focus on it.

   You may find yourself having thoughts about the emotions the situation has brought up and then having thoughts about *those* thoughts. This may bring up even more emotions. Allow yourself to fully explore your feelings, but keep your focus on the original situation you chose.

3. Now, turn to Exercise 6 in your Workbook and list out all the emotions you've experienced. Start each one with "I feel..." If you're new to this, you may struggle to find the words to describe how you feel. You might only identify it as "good" or "bad." Put that down. You might like to explore a list of emotions to inspire you and help you know how each one feels. You'll find an emotions chart in your Workbook to help with this exercise. Over time, you'll find your emotional vocabulary expanding as you become more aware of how each one feels.

4. Once you've finished writing down all the emotions, read your list. As you do, allow yourself to fill up with each emotion. Notice how each one feels without judgment. You may find an emotion becoming more intense as you think about it, or it may quickly pass. Don't try to control them. Simply watch what's happening with each one.

5. When you've finished working through the list, write down your observations in your journal.

GRATITUDE JOURNALING

Gratitude journaling involves writing down the things you are grateful for. You might like to start the day with the good things in your life to put you in a positive mood. You could journal in the evening with a list of things you're grateful for that happened during the day. Or you could do like I do and do both!

The simplest form of gratitude journaling is to write a list of 3-5 things (or more if you like) you're grateful for:

- I'm grateful for my friends
- I'm grateful for my cat
- I'm grateful the sun was shining today

If you want to take it up a notch, add the reasons why you're grateful:

- I'm grateful for my friends because they're always there for me
- I'm grateful for my cat because his fur feels so soft
- I'm grateful the sun was shining today because I love the warmth on my skin

Another approach is to choose a topic and write about it. Think about the things you have in your life and choose one to explore all the reasons you're grateful for them.

You could write about:

- Your family

- Your friends
- Your relationships
- Your body
- Your home
- Your career
- Your hobbies
- The place where you live

I've included this powerful journal activity in your Workbook as part of the 35-day program.

USING JOURNAL PROMPTS

If you find it hard to start, you can always try writing on a journaling prompt. You'll find this list in your Workbook, so you can try a few out right now:

- What was an obstacle you overcame? What did you learn from the experience?
- What is your favorite childhood memory? What do you love about it?
- Write about a time someone did something kind for you. How did that make you feel?
- What is a difficult situation you're dealing with at the moment? How can you be grateful for it?
- How can you view your challenges as opportunities?

- What's something/someone you take for granted that you feel grateful for? How can you show that appreciation?

- What are your strengths/talents? Why are you grateful for them?

- What is a quote you find inspirational? Why do you like that quote?

- What life lessons did you learn from your parents/caregivers? How have they affected your life, good or bad? How can you be grateful for them?

- Who is the teacher or mentor you've had that's inspired you the most?

Honestly, if you can only put one thing into practice right now, I'd recommend journaling. I've learned so much about myself through my journaling practice. I also feel it's made me a better person and helped me be more positive about my ADHD. At the back of your Workbook, I've included a week's worth of journal pages to get you started.

I couldn't have made all this progress by myself, though. You've noticed I refer to my therapist a lot in this book. She's helped me in more ways than I can count, and because of her, I have a lot of tools at my disposal. I want to share some of the more therapy-focused approaches with you. I've found them really helpful, and I know you will, too.

Turn to the next chapter to learn about Cognitive Behavioral Therapy and Dialectical Behavioral Therapy.

THERAPY TECHNIQUES TAILORED FOR YOU

CBT And DBT Strategies For ADHD Minds

"The happiness of your life depends on the quality of your thoughts."

— Marcus Aurelius

> *I wasn't diagnosed with ADHD until I was 42. By this point, I was an absolute mess. I felt so angry. I had spent years being told I was "just" depressed. I "just" had anxiety. Maybe if the so-called professionals had realized I had ADHD, I wouldn't be depressed or anxious!*
>
> *I went into a deep tailspin after my diagnosis. CBT is what helped pull me out. It taught me how to break the cycle of negative thinking. I still have my bad days. CBT is the one thing that helps me get out of those deep holes of depression. – Hatty D.*

HOW CAN I HELP?

Obviously, this book is not designed to replace proper therapeutic interactions. However, based on my own experience and observations, I know that many people don't get the assistance they need because therapy can seem unapproachable when you're not familiar with it, or you simply may not have the funds or insurance cover.

In the next few chapters, I'd like to share some information about the two modalities that I have direct experience with that have helped me greatly.

I hope this will equip you with the awareness to make either or both of them part of your ADHD toolkit without the common access constraints that can often prevent us from benefiting from therapeutic assistance.

WHAT IS CBT?

CBT stands for Cognitive Behavioral Therapy. It's a form of talking therapy used to treat various issues, including ADHD. It deals with how thoughts, beliefs, and attitudes impact your emotions and behavior.

CBT is awesome for helping me shut up my inner critic. I put myself down so much, and CBT is helping me pick myself back up. – Selina K.

CBT works because how we think about things affects how we feel and behave.[1] So, if your ADHD causes you to think negatively about situations, this could make you feel negative emotions. Those bad feelings, in turn, can prompt you to behave in a way that makes things worse. CBT brings together two types of therapy to deal with those thoughts and behaviors in a more positive way:

- Cognitive therapy to explore how you think.
- Behavior therapy to look at what you do.

DO I HAVE TO USE A THERAPIST?

There are many resources available that make it simpler for you to practice CBT by yourself. In addition, you'll find helpful resources in your Workbook, including CBT worksheets that I personally use.

You could also discuss with your healthcare team about whether doing CBT for yourself could be useful. They might:

- Show you where you can access online CBT services.

- Suggest books that can support a CBT approach.

- Provide you with worksheets or other resources you can try out.

I was skeptical about CBT, but after trying it, I found that it really worked. What I found most surprising was how it helped me get more organized. Being late always made me feel terrible. Working with those emotions, I was able to find ways of managing my time that worked for me. And I could be kinder to myself on days when I just couldn't get myself together. It was a game-changer. – Erika A.

WHAT ARE CBT THERAPY SESSIONS LIKE?

If you decide to work with a therapist, you'll pinpoint negative thoughts and behaviors together and find better ways of doing things. You might examine what's going on in your life right now and see how past experiences have shaped you.

I always found life overwhelming. All I could see were all the things I couldn't do. CBT helped me split my goals into manageable chunks and take steps towards them. It was amazing how those little achievements added up. Suddenly, I felt like I wasn't a failure anymore. – Polly H.

During a CBT session, you might:

- Look at what you've done in earlier sessions and look at your progress.

- Do exercises with your therapist to learn about your thoughts, emotions, and behavior.

- Agree about what you'll work on outside of therapy.

Outside sessions, you may have tasks to do, like filling out worksheets or keeping a journal.

While many women with ADHD find CBT invaluable, it doesn't work for everyone. That doesn't mean there's anything wrong with you. It could be that your therapist wasn't a good fit. Or it might be that you'd do better with a different approach. Many people who don't get on with CBT find that DBT is more effective.

WHAT IS DBT?

Dialectical Behavior Therapy (DBT) is another form of talking therapy. It is based on CBT but designed specifically for those of us who feel our emotions more intensely. "Dialectical" means seeing how two opposing concepts can be true at the same time. In this instance, you are moving towards self-acceptance while working to change negative behavior patterns. This might seem contradictory, but they are both possible.

DBT aims to support you as you:

- Learn more about your difficult feelings and accept them.

- Practice ways of managing those emotions.

- Be able to implement positive changes in your life.

After a few months of practicing DBT, I didn't feel that my ADHD symptoms had changed much. But looking at things, I realized I was much better at managing how they affected me. I could get through a day without yet another ADHD crisis. I could stay on top of my emotions instead of them consuming me. – Phoebe C.

DBT isn't for everyone. It's more likely to suit you if you prefer to focus on the present and future rather than the past

CAN I DO DBT BY MYSELF?

Some people find it difficult to grasp DBT methods without support. However, you'll see from the techniques outlined in this book that it's not as hard as you might think. I'll cover some of the most popular DBT take-home methods that I've learned and used in Chapter 10, including ACCEPTS and DEARMAN. The most important thing is that you make a commitment to yourself to put into practice what you learn.

Starting with just one technique will make it easier for you to implement it. Add more as you become comfortable with the modality.

WHAT DOES DBT WITH A THERAPIST LOOK LIKE?

Approaches to DBT can vary depending on your therapist and where you live. Typically, a course will usually include:

- Pre-treatment where you and your therapist determine whether DBT is right for you.

- 1:1 sessions lasting 45-60 minutes. These sessions aim to reduce the impact of your ADHD symptoms, minimize behavior that might interfere with therapy, help you set and achieve goals, and replace negative behaviors with more helpful ones. You may be asked to keep a diary between sessions to track your emotions and behavior.

- Group skill training where you learn practical skills to use in your everyday life. You are likely to cover mindfulness (which we look at in detail later in this book), how to cope with stress, interpersonal skills, and emotional regulation.

- You may also receive support from telephone coaching between sessions. If you need some extra help, this is an option where you'll have short 5-15-minute calls with your therapist.

I used to fight against my emotions for so long. Now I know they're not a negative thing. They're there to help me. I still feel my emotions very intensely, but now I know what they are. I can manage them without them causing me problems. – Liz S.

Your DBT therapist will use a combination of acceptance and change techniques. You will learn to better understand yourself so you know why you do certain things. You will also discover how to replace harmful behavior with a more supportive approach.

Now you know a little more about what all those letters mean! In the next chapter, we're going to take some of the tools taught by

CBT and DBT and show how you can use them to find empowerment in your ADHD experience.

Before you move on, please spend a moment with Exercise 9 in your Workbook, where you'll find the CBT worksheets I've included. Let's do this together! Could you share your experience with CBT in the LearnWell Community?

BE YOUR OWN THERAPIST

Customizing CBT And DBT Techniques For Your Unique Experience

"We cannot solve our problems with the same thinking we used when we created them."

– Albert Einstein

"I don't need any help! I can do it myself!"

I couldn't help but smile as I watched my four-year-old niece trying to carry an armful of toys without dropping them. Highly independent from an early age, I could see much of myself in her. I always insisted I could do everything for myself. I didn't need any help.

The only thing was that I was wrong. I desperately needed help. It was all bravado. Anyone looking at me could easily see I was a mess. I was impulsive, emotional, and disorganized. Looking back, I don't know why it was so important to me to pretend I was okay. I could have saved myself years of heartache if I'd been open to help sooner. It's one of the reasons I wrote this book. I wanted to help others so they wouldn't have to endure all the pain, bullying, and disappointments I faced.

Years of therapy have equipped me with a range of tools that make it easier for me to cope. I want to focus on some of the ones I use most. Everything I'm about to give you, I learned either through CBT or DBT.

PROBLEM-SOLVING FOR ADHD WOMEN

I know, I know. Everyone has problems. For people who don't have ADHD, life isn't automatically easy.

But when you do have ADHD, it can make it difficult to find solutions to problems. Our issues with emotional regulation make us easily frustrated and angry when something goes wrong. When emotions are high, problem-solving skills are low. Alternatively, we can stick our heads in the sand and hope whatever it is will go away.¹

Our organization problems mean that even if we are able to stay calm in the face of challenges, we may not have a clue where to start fixing things. Procrastination can kick in. It's too much to deal with. Better not to deal with it at all, right? Even when we can get going on a solution, if something isn't interesting, we're unlikely to stick with it.²

> *I can stay hyper-focused for hours on a difficult cross-stitch pattern. But my car's making a weird noise? I might mean to sort it out, but it's just not a high priority. I only tend to get to it when my car's died completely. And then I've got to find hundreds for a mechanic because heck if I'm going to sort it. – Vicki N.*

CBT helped me develop strategies to cope when a problem comes up. Here are six steps I find helpful when problem-solving:

Life Will Regularly Serve You Lemons

1. Recognize and accept that there will be problems in life. This might seem obvious, but when you consciously accept that you'll need to deal with problems at some point, it helps you be less reactive or procrastinate. You're already prepared to take action.

Remember To Breathe

2. Pause. You don't have to deal with the problem right away. If your ADHD makes you reactive, it's a particularly good idea to give yourself some space to be calm before you dive into it. Set a time limit that feels appropriate. When the time's up, you'll deal with it. *After* you've given yourself room to breathe.

Can You Fix It? It's Okay If You Can't!

3. Decide if you really need to fix it. Not all problems need solving. Sometimes, it might make more sense to accept that that's simply how things are. This is especially useful if there's nothing you can do to change something or you know you don't have the time or energy to deal with it. Accepting a situation doesn't mean you have to like it, but it does mean you're making a conscious choice not to waste time and energy on it.

One Step At A Time

4. Remember, problem-solving is a process. If you decide you do need to fix it, remind yourself that the solution might take time, even if you don't like it. Being patient is a toughie for ADHD women. We like things to be sorted NOW! When that's not possible, we can start stressing about the problem. We get caught up in what if we don't fix it or what if we fail. We think ourselves into inaction. Let that worry go. Focus it on the problem at hand. And if you're taking a pause from finding a solution, don't use that time to worry instead.

Get Help

5. Nobody can do everything alone. Seeking support from someone you know could help find a solution. Be kind to yourself. You may need to talk about how you feel before you get stuck in. The situation could be making you feel emotional. Give yourself the grace of acknowledging your emotions so you're ready to tackle the issue.

Now You Can Get Started

6. Be prepared to do the work. Once you've found the people who can help you with your problem, you can identify the steps you need to take – and take them! Stay focused on the solution. Ask yourself:

    - What do I want to achieve?
    - What would a solution look like?
    - Why is finding this solution important to me?
    - How will having the solution change things for me?
    - What steps do I need to take to get to the solution?

This process might seem long, but in practice, I've found it streamlines things. I could either spend time working through the six steps or stressing and reacting. Guess which one makes more sense?

Is there a problem you are facing right now? In your Workbook, there is space to work through that problem using these six steps. Again, they are:

1. Remember – there will be problems.
2. Breathe.
3. Decide if it can be fixed.
4. Understand that it might take time.
5. Get help.
6. Do the work.

You'll find that writing things out will help you look at the situation more objectively and help you take action to resolve things. Remember, you don't have to fix things by yourself. If it would be helpful to get someone else involved, whether it's a friend or a professional, include asking them for support in your steps towards a solution.

COGNITIVE RESTRUCTURING

Cognitive restructuring involves actively changing the way you think. This is something you'll find a lot in DBT. Several different strategies can help you develop a more positive mindset.

Self-monitor

If you want to change a negative thought pattern, you must first see where it starts. Become a conscious observer of your thoughts. What makes you feel negative? What puts you in a negative state of mind? Also, consider when and where these thoughts come up. You may find that certain places or situations are more likely to disrupt how you view things. You can then be ready for them in the future. I found journaling particularly good for this.

Question assumptions

We tend to think our thoughts are automatically true. After all, we're thinking them, so they must be!

In reality, thoughts are just thoughts. They're not necessarily true or objective. Get in the habit of questioning them, especially if they're holding you back.

If an unhelpful thought comes up, ask yourself:

- Is this thought based in fact or coming from my emotions?
- Is there any evidence that this thought is correct?
- Is there any evidence that this thought is incorrect?
- How can I test my assumptions?
- How else could I interpret the information this thought is based on?
- Is the situation black and white, or is it more nuanced?

You'll find a section in your Workbook with space to practice this approach. Think of a negative thought you had recently that made you feel bad about yourself. Then, go through the questions to see whether this thought is valid. If you can think of even one example in your life to prove the thought is incorrect, you know it's untrue, and you can reframe it.

As you get into the habit of questioning your assumptions, you will get better at recognizing when a thought is helpful or not. When you see something isn't helping you, you'll be able to turn your focus to more supportive thoughts.

Do A Cost-Benefit Analysis

It might sound strange to do a cost-benefit analysis of your thoughts, but it really helped me. Considering the pros and cons of a particular way of thinking made it easy for me to let go of ideas I'd held for years.

You'll need to write your answers down. You'll find space in your Workbook for this. Choose a thought and ask yourself:

- What do I get out of this thought? (Let's say you beat yourself up for being silly. How does calling yourself silly benefit you?)
- What does this thought cost you regarding emotions, time, energy, etc?
- How does this thought affect you long-term?
- How does this thought affect the people who deal with you?
- How does this thought help or hinder your goals?

Once you have a visible list of the costs and benefits of a thought, you can make an informed decision to replace it with something new. If you've been putting yourself down for a while, you might find it difficult to immediately replace it with a positive thought. But you can start correcting yourself by thinking, "I'm doing my best. I'm getting better." Can't you?

Find Alternatives

Question everything about your thoughts. Is there a different way of viewing things? Is your version of the truth the only one?

Let's say you go into a room and think the people in there are talking about you. How do you know that? What could they have been talking about instead? If they were talking about you, could they have been saying nice things?

The more alternative explanations you can think of, the easier it becomes to see that, most of the time, things aren't as bad as we think. It's our thoughts that make things worse. They can misinterpret things or even invent situations that don't exist.

You might find it helpful to come up with some positive affirmations you can repeat to yourself when you find these unhelpful thoughts coming up. Some examples could be:

- I work hard.
- I always do my best.
- I have valuable contributions to make.
- I have lots of positive qualities.
- I have skills and talents.
- I view the world differently to most people. I see things others don't.

Choose one and get into the habit of saying it every time you notice those unhelpful thoughts. You might like to keep a tally of how many times you need to say your affirmation. While the number might be high at first, as you get into the habit of thinking more positively and using your affirmation, you'll find the amount you need to say your affirmation decreases.

The list above has also been repeated in your Workbook with space for you to run this exercise.

These techniques have been a real game changer for me. At first, I didn't understand how viewing things differently could change reality. Different thoughts weren't going to get me a pay rise or a nicer apartment!

The funny thing is, they have. Being more positive and understanding of myself has made me more effective at work – which did get me that pay rise. That extra money has helped me move to a bigger place.

This is such a powerful subject that I wanted to spend a little more time discussing it. So, we will look at a few more techniques in the next chapter. Read on to find out all about them.

10

THE MOOD RESET BUTTON

5 Quick Emotional Regulation Techniques

"When you change the way you look at things, the things you look at change."

– Wayne Dyer

> *You could say DBT saved my life. I was at an emotional breaking point. My relationship fell to pieces, and I went with it. I'm not ashamed to say that I considered ending things. I'd tried to be 'normal' and failed miserably. What was the point of anything?*
>
> *Luckily, my dear friend E. stepped in before I did anything stupid. She found a therapist she thought I might like and even drove me to my first session to make sure I went.*
>
> *My therapist specialized in DBT. I felt a bit stupid when I first started doing the work at home. I didn't see how being more mindful was going to help. Life sucked! Wouldn't being more aware of it make things even worse?*
>
> *But gradually, I started to notice that it was making things that little bit easier. Then my therapist told me he thought I had ADHD. When I got my diagnosis, everything made sense. I was able to adapt what I was learning from DBT to how my brain worked. Everything's completely different now. I'm so glad I'm still here to share my story.* – Carrie M.

TIPP

If you're feeling like Carrie did, TIPP is the tool you need. It's designed to help you get through times when you feel like it's all too much.

TIPP HAS FOUR STAGES

Temperature

We can physically feel hot when we're upset. TIPP starts with cooling you down by splashing cold water on your face, holding an ice cube, or standing in front of an AC unit. Cooling down physically will help cool down your emotional heat as well.

Intense Exercise

Intense emotions are matched by intense exercise. Do what works within your physical capabilities. Run to the end of your yard and back a few times. Do jumping jacks until you're too tired to do more. Swim some laps in the pool. This will help increase the flow of oxygen in your body, bringing down your stress levels.

Paced Breathing

Practice breathing exercises to control your emotions. We covered a few in Chapter Four. You can choose one of those techniques or use another breathing technique you prefer.

Paired Muscle Relaxation

This involves choosing a group of muscles, e.g. the muscles in your arms, tightening them for five seconds, and then letting all that tension go. The muscles become more relaxed than before. This needs less oxygen, slowing your breathing and heart rate.

Working through the four steps of TIPP helps you enter a state of mind where you can make good choices and cope with whatever you face. I've included the TIPP exercise in your Workbook to help you practice but also as an easy reference to turn to when you're feeling hot and bothered.

ACCEPTS

Our ADHD brains can go into overdrive. Say the boss has asked you to see her later. You spend the whole time before your meeting panicking. Is it a good meeting or a bad meeting? Was it something you did?

ACCEPTS helps you deal with those times when your emotions are running wild. It lets you function until you can solve the problem.

THERE ARE SEVEN STEPS TO ACCEPTS

Activities

Do something interesting and healthy to keep you busy and occupied. You may have found your ADHD naturally does this for you. Ever find yourself cleaning out a cupboard when you should be filling out your tax return? That's your mind distracting you from the stress of facing all that paperwork. It's ACCEPTS in action!

Contributing

Do something nice for someone. Performing an act of service has multiple benefits. It makes the recipient happy, it makes us feel good about ourselves, and it takes your mind off what's bothering you while you do something useful.

Comparisons

Have you been through a more difficult situation than now? What was it? (If you haven't, TIPP may be more helpful right now.) Is there someone worse off than you? Are you home, warm, safe, and fed, while someone else is piecing their life together after a natural disaster? Getting perspective can help you realize that this will pass and you'll survive like you have all those other times.

Emotions

Find a way to provoke the opposite feeling from how you are right now. If you're stressed, meditate. If you're depressed, look up funny videos online. Bringing in the opposite emotion helps counter your current feelings.

Push Away

If you just can't face something right now it's okay to put it to one side for a while. Push it away with activities, thinking about other subjects, or mindfulness. If it's helpful, set a timer to come back. Knowing you'll get to it when you're ready helps you to relax in the meantime.

Thoughts

Distract your mind by keeping it busy. Recite the alphabet backward. Do a crossword or Sudoku puzzle. Keeping your mind occupied helps you take the edge off strong emotions until you can emotionally regulate.

Sensation

Do something to soothe each of your five senses. Take a warm bath with sweet-smelling oils. Put on relaxing music. Have a tasty snack. Watch a movie you like wrapped up in a soft blanket. These comforting activities will help you cope with what's happening.

RADICAL ACCEPTANCE

Grant me the serenity to accept the things I cannot change; courage to change the things I can; and the wisdom to know the difference. – Serenity Prayer

There are some things we may not like about our lives but can't do anything to change. Accepting them will help you feel more at peace and able to function.

I found that my ADHD diagnosis allowed me to accept that there were things about myself I wasn't going to be able to change. I might not like how hard I find it to function sometimes, but beating myself up about it DOES NOT help.

Radical acceptance includes accepting that we have ADHD. It makes some things harder for us. We have challenges other people couldn't even imagine. But we can use the skills in this book to help us stay calm and do our best. Accepting our circumstances means we can work within them. We then get to play to our strengths instead of focusing on our weaknesses. We've got so much to offer the world. It's time to unleash our superpowers!

TIPP and ACCEPTS are more about coping with stress rather than dealing with stressful situations. DBT offers other tools for handling those problems. One of the most useful is interpersonal effectiveness.

INTERPERSONAL EFFECTIVENESS SKILLS

Interpersonal effectiveness enables you to get other people to meet your needs, do what you need them to do, and take you seriously. It helps you strengthen your existing relationships, forge healthy new ones, and cut yourself off from unhealthy or toxic relationships.

While they come more naturally to some than others, interpersonal effectiveness is learned. This is great news. It means that while you might have to work a little harder, you *can* master these skills. DBT is particularly good for helping with this. It utilizes some of these skill-building activities:

DEARMAN SKILL

DEARMAN is an acronym for a process that helps you build better relationships. It has seven steps:

- Describe the current situation. Stay factual without bringing in emotions. Tell the other person what has brought you here.
- Express how you feel about it. Don't assume the other person is a mind reader. They need to be told how you feel.

- Assert yourself. Ask for what you want or say that you won't do something. Be explicit. Remember – there's no mindreading in this process!

- Reinforce the rewards for the other person by detailing the positive consequences of fulfilling your needs. If need be, also lay out what the negative consequences will be if they're not met.

- Mindfully stay focused on your end goal. Don't let yourself get distracted or drawn off-topic. Use the broken record technique[1]. Keep repeating yourself and ignore any insults, attacks, threats, or attempts to change the subject.

- Appear confident, even if you're not feeling it. Keep your voice and body language strong. Maintain eye contact. Hold your ground.

- Negotiate. You may need to concede a little to get what you want. Be open to offers or alternative solutions. The most important thing is you get what you need. How you get there is less important.

GIVE SKILL

This is another way of building positive relationships with effective communication.

- (Be) Gentle. Avoid verbal threats, attacks, or abuse. State what will happen if you don't get what you need, but without hyperbole or drama.

- (Act) Interested. Don't interrupt the other person, and listen to them with the same respect you want for yourself. If they need to take some time to prepare for a conversation, give them the space they need. Take it as an opportunity to get yourself mentally prepared.

- Validate. Demonstrate that you understand the other person's opinions and thoughts. If you observe something that needs action, follow through. For example, if someone wants to talk in private, take your conversation elsewhere. If they're busy, schedule a time that will work for both of you.

- (Use an) Easy manner. Ditch the attitude. Smile. Be approachable. Don't be afraid to use humor where appropriate.

FAST SKILL

This allows you to be open and honest about your problems:

- (Be) Fair, both to yourself and to the person you're communicating with. Both your feelings are valid.

- (Don't over) Apologize. Never apologize for who you are or for taking up space. You are allowed an opinion. You're allowed to disagree. No is a complete sentence!

- Stick to your values. Don't sell yourself out to make someone else happy. Be clear on what you feel is the moral, right way – and see it through.

- (Be) Truthful. Be honest, even if it feels hard. Don't exaggerate the situation or make excuses. The truth is more than enough.

It might seem unnatural at first to take a FAST approach or use TIPP in the heat of the moment. The more you practice these methods, the more natural they'll feel. They'll soon become second nature, especially when you see their impact.

Set yourself the challenge of taking a DEARMAN approach next time you have a problem to solve. Prepare yourself for that moment right now by turning to your Workbook. You'll find some space to write about what you think would happen based on how you used to deal with situations. Then, write what would be an ideal solution if you took a DEARMAN approach.

When a problem comes up, revisit what you wrote. Now add to it by detailing what could happen if you acted how you've always done in the past. Consider how things could change if you took a DEARMAN approach and use that to prepare you for dealing with the other person. After you've spoken to them, come back and write down how it went. How is it different? How could you improve things even further? There is space for all of this in your Workbook.

I've saved the best for last with this section. We'll examine mindfulness, the simple approach that's taking the therapeutic world by storm and changing the lives of women with ADHD. Turn to the next chapter to see how it works.

11

MINDFULNESS FOR THE ACTIVE MIND

Practical Methods For ADHD Brains

"Life gives you plenty of time to do whatever you want to do if you stay in the present moment."

– Deepak Chopra

Mornings were always the worst time for me. I'd dread the blaring alarm, dragging me out of what was never enough sleep. I'd hit the snooze button again and again, deluding myself I could delay the start of the day. Instead, I'd sabotage myself by making myself late.

Getting ready was a mad panic. My brain never fully came online until I was at work behind my desk, the first cup of coffee safely behind me. So, when my therapist suggested being more mindful about my mornings, I could barely stop myself laughing.

But when she explained what it could do for me, I figured it couldn't hurt to try it. And wow. Just wow.

When you go through life without thinking about how you'd like things to be, you become more reactive. And when you're reactive from ADHD in the first place, this is the last thing you need. When you take a few minutes to ground yourself into the present moment, you can be more mindful and approach life in a far more constructive way.

The number of Google searches for "mindfulness" has increased by a factor of almost ten over the last 20 years[1]. People have started to wake up to the fact that mindfulness can help you become:

- Less stressed.
- More satisfied with your life.
- Better at relationships across the board.
- A higher performer

- Healthier.[2]

If you thought mindfulness involved time alone, a quiet, safe space, a yoga mat or meditation cushion, and hours of lessons to master it, think again. Mindfulness simply means being in the present moment without worrying about the future or stressing about the past. Staying focused on what's happening right now frees you from the ways your mind can try to undermine you.

Here are a few simple ways to be mindful in your life right now. All it takes is a few minutes throughout the day.

WAKE UP MINDFULLY WITH AN INTENTION FOR THE DAY

Make this the first thing you do every morning before reaching for your phone. You don't even have to get out of bed for it!

1. Sit or lie comfortably in your bed (or sit on a chair) and close your eyes.

2. Take three deep, easy breaths, breathing in through your nose and out through the mouth. Then, watch your breath for a few cycles as it relaxes into its own rhythm.

3. Ask yourself:
   - What is my intention for this day?
   - How can I show up today to be my best self?
   - What qualities do I want to work on?
   - How can I take better care of myself?

- How can I show more compassion to others and myself?
- What will make me feel fulfilled today?

4. Once you have answered these questions, use them to inspire you to set your intention. For example, if you said you wanted to work on being kinder to yourself, you might say, "Today, I will show myself grace and understanding." Choose whatever works for you.

5. Throughout the day, check in with yourself and see how you're aligning with your intention. Take a few moments to close your eyes, take a breath, and remind yourself of your intention. The more this becomes part of your daily routine, the more you'll notice how your mood improves, making it easier to work with your ADHD symptoms.

Your workbook has space to answer the questions in step 3. Use it to help you choose some intentions in advance for those times when choosing a new intention feels like too much, such as first thing in the morning.

MINDFUL EATING

You can do this with every meal or pick one that will be the focus for your day. When you eat mindfully, meals become food for the mind, body, and soul.

1. Before you start to eat, close your eyes and turn your attention to your breath. Take 8-10 deep breaths to bring you into the present moment.

When you eat mindfully, meals become food for the mind, body, and soul

2. Ask yourself, "On a scale of 1-10, how hungry am I?" What physical sensations are you noticing that tell you whether you're hungry or not? Is your stomach growling? Is your mouth watering? Or are you feeling nothing? Listen to what your body is telling you rather than following what you think you should be doing.

3. Now you know how hungry you really are, you can eat more mindfully to meet your needs. Stop when you are full, even if you haven't finished everything.

4. Pay attention to every bite. Smell your food before tasting it. Chew more slowly. Notice how the food feels when you first put it in your mouth. How does that change as you eat it? Really savor the moment.

5. If you don't love it, don't do it. With your first three mindful bites, consider how much you enjoy the taste, flavor, and texture. Does your body love it? Did you really need to eat or is it a habit? What is it about that food that's making you feel that way? Is it filling an emotional need or is it genuinely nourishing you? If you're comfort eating, is there a healthier alternative? You can use this understanding of your body's reactions to help you nurture yourself more mindfully in the future.

This exercise is also in your Workbook as part of the 35-day program. It's a great practice that you can use often to turn a mundane activity into a mindfulness exercise. Who knew you could learn so much about yourself just by eating?

MINDFULLY REWIRE YOUR BRAIN

We spend most of our lives on autopilot, lurching from one task to the next without really thinking about what we're doing. Mindfulness encourages us to slow down. We can be more conscious when we take our time. Bizarrely, I've noticed I get more done since I started to go slow!

Here are some ways to help rewire your brain more mindfully:

1. **Get in your own way.** If there's something you want to do, like yoga or meditation, put your mat or cushion right in the middle of the room so you trip over it when you walk past.

2. **Redo your reminders.** All these wonderful new intentions are great. You may well decide to put sticky notes everywhere to remind you about them. You'll probably find it works for a while, but then you slide back into old habits. In Chapter Five, I took you through how to set up your daily checklist with reminders for regular tasks. Rewrite your reminders every week. Make them different each time with doodles or notes so they stay in your mind.

3. **Write some "if/then" rules.** Bring mindfulness into your routine with some simple rules at certain checkpoints. So, you might say, "If the phone rings, take a deep breath before responding."

If you really feel you need it, there are lots of mindfulness classes around to help you get started with this powerful practice. But as you can see from this chapter, it's easy to be more mindful in everything you do.

Now, it's time to move on to the next part of this book. You're going to learn how to get through your day-to-day life regardless of the obstacles your ADHD throws in the way.

PART 3

Optimizing Daily Life

12

TIME MASTERY FOR ADHD

Strategies For Productivity And Punctuality

"Time is really the only capital a human being has, and the only thing he can't afford to lose."

– Thomas Edison

You're so lazy!

 You just need to try harder!

 Everyone else can get here on time. Why can't you?

I've always struggled to be on time. It's like I know what the numbers on a clock mean, but I can't figure out why they change so quickly! I plan out my day, but everything takes so much longer than I expect. I end up falling behind, but I don't notice until it's too late.

 It turns out that "time blindness" is a common ADHD trait. While I understand that time passes, I find it hard to prioritize my time. I have no idea how long it's going to take me to do something, and when I do have a good idea, I forget to take into account other factors that might put me behind. – Samantha G.

It wasn't until I got my diagnosis that I could finally stop blaming myself for all those latenesses. I've implemented a number of strategies that have really helped, and I'm sharing them with you so you don't have to be late anymore.

KEEP AN EYE ON TIME – LITERALLY

ADHD makes it difficult for you to understand the notion of time.[1] Make it easy on yourself by using lots of external reminders.

Start by putting up timepieces where you can easily see them – clocks on the wall, a watch on your wrist, an alarm clock by the bed. Analog clocks are actually better for this than digital because you can see time traveling around the clock with the hands.

In Chapter Five, I took you through my Daily Checklist. I want to use the topic of Time Management to reinforce the importance of that tool. If you haven't done so already, please refer back to the Checklist I provided in your Workbook and complete at least one day where you set out your tasks and add the time you expect each task to take. Adding the 'duration' to each task makes the process very effective.

This activity will create a profound shift in your feeling of control over your day and your appreciation of how you can manage time around your tasks.

BREAK TASKS DOWN INTO SMALLER TASKS

It can feel overwhelming when you have a lot to do. When you can't imagine how you're going to get it all done, you don't know where to start. So then you get **nothing** done, and you're even more overwhelmed.

When you're creating your Daily Schedule, break your tasks down into manageable pieces. Unless you've got a looming deadline, you don't have to finish a task in one go. Give yourself a certain amount of time to focus on something you need to do. Focus on getting that first part of it done. If you have time left afterward, you can move on to the next part. If not, you've still made progress instead of spending a day distracting yourself from a big task that feels like an overwhelming mountain.

REGULARLY UPDATE YOUR TO-DO LIST

Your to-do list informs your Daily Checklist. There will be things on your to-do list that you need to remember to do at some point but won't include on your Daily Schedule. You'll lose track if you try to remember them by yourself. Then you get stressed because you forget important things and even more stressed because you'll forget everything else as well.

Something that's really worked for me is to get a notebook for all my tasks. I know people who prefer to use a whiteboard and wipe out tasks they've finished. Another option is to have a document on your phone in a notes app.

I like using a paper notebook. There's something about writing out all my tasks by hand that helps me focus on what matters. I update it at the start of the week with everything I need to do, adding to it if something new comes up. I've included a version of this Master To-Do List in your Workbook.

When I update my list, I write the days I will do a task next to the most important ones. I come back to my master list every morning when I'm putting together my Checklist. I cross off the tasks I completed the day before, which gives me such a real sense of achievement.

This process keeps me focused. I can see at a glance how much I've done. It makes me feel less of a failure because I'm making progress I can actually see.

KNOW YOUR PATTERNS

Think about those times when you were on fire and in the zone.

- What time of day was it?
- What were you doing?
- Were there any similarities between those times?

The more aware you are of when you're at your best, the more you can use that to manage your time most effectively. Put the most important or challenging tasks when you're at your peak.

DECIDE HOW LONG SOMETHING WILL TAKE – THEN DOUBLE IT

People with ADHD often struggle to know how long it will take to do something.[2] I'm always surprised by how long something takes me to do. That's why however long you think something will take, double it. You could even triple it. It makes your Daily Checklist more realistic and achievable. If you have time left over, you can get something else done. (But you probably won't!)

Also, build in some buffer time. When I realized it took me 15 minutes to leave the house, I started telling myself I needed to leave 15 minutes sooner than I did. Thinking I must get out at 7.45 means I'm still on time when I finally make it out at 8.

I can't promise you'll always be on time after this. But I have found that all these tips have really helped me stay on top of my schedule. People complain about how bad I am at timekeeping a lot less.

Now we've organized your time, we can move onto organizing your space. This will really help you feel more in control of your life.

13

FROM CHAOS TO ORDER

Simple Organization Techniques

"Cleaning and organizing is a practice, not a project." – Meagan Francis

"You'd lose your head if it wasn't screwed on," joked my best friend, Lyn, as I scrabbled about in my bag for my keys.

She thought it was funny, but it was no joke to me. I was notorious for misplacing everything. Glasses, keys, phone… Lyn was right. I probably *would* lose my head if it wasn't screwed on!

DBT therapy helped me learn ways of organizing my space. I wouldn't say I'm perfect, but Lyn doesn't joke about me losing things anymore.

Everyone has times when they're disorganized. You don't have to have ADHD to find it difficult to get organized. But if you are neurodiverse, organization is a skill that feels almost impossible to master.[1] We get easily distracted, so we can start tidying and abandon it for something else. It's difficult to find the motivation to get back into it, so the mess just builds up. I used to have a clean clothes pile and a dirty laundry pile. That was my idea of organization. The number of times I got the two messed up doesn't bear thinking about!

Organization needs focus, discipline, and motivation, all things that are challenging when you have ADHD.[2] But if you can manage this important skill, it can help alleviate some of your ADHD symptoms. Even if you only make a few small changes to your habits, you'll find it really helps.

Here are a few tips to get you started.

A PLACE FOR EVERYTHING AND EVERYTHING IN ITS PLACE

I've lost track of how much time I've spent looking for my keys or glasses, only to find them exactly where I'd left them. Now, I have specific places to keep my important items. You might like to have a hook or bowl for your keys and always put them there as soon as you get home. Have a specific place where you always keep your wallet. If you leave it in your purse, have a place where you always put your purse. If you're using notepads for your schedules or journaling, keep them in the same place. Mine are all on my nightstand.

When you put your things in the same place all the time, you're less likely to lose them.

You might also find it helpful to keep similar items together. Chargers and cables can go in one drawer, and important documents can go in another. Keeping related items together makes it easier to find them because they're somewhere that makes sense.

CUT BACK ON CLUTTER

The more stuff you have, the more you have to organize. Decluttering and getting rid of things you don't need anymore leaves you with less to organize. You make the job so much easier with that one step.

You don't have to get rid of everything. If you love something or it makes you happy, keep it, even if it's tucked away in a drawer.

But if you haven't used something in ages or forgotten you had it, it's probably time to get rid of it.

Pick something to organize, like a set of drawers or your wardrobe. Go through each item and be ruthless. Have three piles – keep, donate, throw away. Only keep those things you actually use or absolutely adore. Otherwise, if it's in good condition, donate it to Goodwill. If not, throw it in the trash.

LABEL EVERYTHING

When you've decided where you will keep everything, it's useful to label everything. For example, you might label the drawer with your cables and chargers "Cables/Chargers." This is particularly helpful if you're new to organization and aren't sure you'll remember your system.

This also means that if you need someone to help you, labeling everything makes it easier for others to find things and put them away again.

DO ONE THING AT A TIME

When you have ADHD, you can have a big burst of motivation, decide you're going to organize *everything* then lose your enthusiasm halfway through. This can leave you with a bigger mess than when you started.

Do one thing at a time. If you have a task to get done, remove all distractions so you're not tempted to get your phone out or get stuck into emails. If you're sorting out your house, choose one room, or even one area of the room, to focus on and leave everything else.

Dedicate a different day to tidying different rooms. Monday could be your bedroom day, Tuesday could be for your kitchen, Wednesday could be for the bathroom, and so on. Not only will you not get distracted every time you see something that needs doing in a different room, but you're less overwhelmed when you've only got one room to worry about.

DO THINGS YOUR WAY

Everyone's different. The way I like to organize things might not work for you.

Don't do what other people tell you when it comes to organizing just for the sake of it. If you like to get dressed and undressed in your bedroom, it might be better to keep your laundry basket at the bottom of your bed instead of in the laundry room. If something makes sense to you, don't worry about what anyone else thinks. This is about making life easier for **you.**

LITTLE AND OFTEN

If organization is something you really struggle to do, just do ten minutes of tidying at a time. Ten minutes every day will add up quickly. Once you've sorted out one area, you shouldn't need to spend so much time on it in the future. Do one drawer or cupboard at a time or one corner of a room. You'll get there in the end.

In your Workbook, I've put together a simple "Get Organized" exercise to quickly improve your organization. You can complete it as a part of the 35-day program or come back to it for a quick spruce up of your space when things feel out of hand.

Oh, and please share your organizational tips in the LearnWell Community!

We've organized your time and space. Now, it's time to consider how you can establish routines to help you turn your new systems into a way of life and avoid reverting to old habits.

14

CREATING HELPFUL HABITS

How To Build Routines That Stick

"You'll never change your life until you change something you do daily. The secret of your success is found in your daily routine."

– John C. Maxwell

"Stay behind after class. We need to talk."

My heart sank at the inevitable lecture ahead.

I knew what this one would be about. I was behind with all my homework.

I knew what I would be told. "You need to create helpful habits that become your routine. Do your homework before you do anything else. Set yourself reminders. Keep a homework diary."

I knew it would be a total waste of time.

Did my teachers really think I hadn't tried it already? Habits and routines made my brain ache. They were overwhelming, a total waste of time.

It's one of the major contradictions about ADHD. Having routines makes it easier to manage your ADHD symptoms. But those very symptoms make it challenging to put them in place. Even when you do have routines you think will work, ADHD tends to leave them by the wayside.

Routines—a collection of helpful habits—make your life simpler. We've covered many ways to build helpful habits, including organizing your time, organizing your space, daily checklists, and scheduling activities. All of these will make your life easier.

But despite all these valuable tools, some people still struggle. So, let's start by looking at why it can go wrong. When you know the problem, it's easier to find the solution.

ROUTINES ARE BORING

Our wonderful ADHD brains love new, shiny things. We are the epitome of spontaneity. Novelty and impulsivity are the antithesis of routine. That's why routines can strike us as dull and pointless.[1]

You can get around this by:

- Make fun a habit. There's no reason why each day can't incorporate things you enjoy doing that give you the motivation to keep going.

    Ask yourself, "What fun thing will I treat myself to?" Use your Workbook to make a list of possible activities that could be part of each day. This could be anything from a walk in the park to a conversation with a friend. Then, add a touch of excitement by throwing a pair of dice to help you pick one at random. You could even use your dice to help you figure out the order you will do your tasks on that day.

- Incorporating positive reinforcement. Some tasks are easier to make more fun than others. Positive reinforcement will help you push through on the ones you don't enjoy as much.

    If you want to get up earlier, ask yourself why. Is it just because everyone says you should? That's not going to cut it. But do you want to do it because you won't be late for work? So you won't have to deal with getting into trouble? Getting up earlier means you'll avoid the stress of rushing. You'll have time for a relaxing cup of coffee instead of grabbing it on the go. That *is* motivating. Give yourself a little reward for getting up on time, whether that be a treat or looking yourself in the mirror and saying, "Great job." You could even arrange with a friend to text each other congratulations for getting up on time!

- Allowing yourself to change your routine. As long as everything gets done, there's no reason the routine around them has to stay the same. The need for change is hard-wired into you, so let that become a habit.

   You could decide that on the first day of the month, you'll create new helpful habits. You could change the order you get ready in the morning. Switch out doing email first thing for organizing your Checklist for the day. Always changing things still gives you structure and satisfies all the contradictions that routines cause for ADHD minds.

You'll find space in your Workbook for brainstorming ways to include positive reinforcement in your routine. This could be anything from having a friend text you congratulations on following through, saying positive affirmations to yourself in the mirror, having a cup of coffee from your favorite coffee shop, playing a game on your phone, or taking a walk. All the things designed to put a smile on your face.

ROUTINES FEEL CONFINING

You may have found routines restricting in the past. But they should do the opposite. They should free you up for more of what you love.

You can get over this by:

- Changing your perspective. Remind yourself that a routine removes a lot of the decisions and choices that overwhelm you into inaction. Helpful habits eliminate the need to think about what to do next. Laying your clothes out the night before means you don't have to frantically find something to wear in the morning. Keeping your keys in the same place means you don't have to hunt for them before you can leave.

- Not trying too much. Routines don't have to be a big deal. Start small and gradually add to it. What part of the day needs the most attention? Preparing for work? Hitting deadlines? Organizing your Checklist? Get your work things ready the night before? Create a timeline of tasks that need to be done with dates and times? Following the steps in this book to put together a Checklist? Try **one** new habit and see how it works before adding one more.

- Giving it time. It can be hard to see your progress when you're right in the middle. You can give up too soon if you think something isn't working.

Whatever habit you're trying to introduce, give it a week. At the end of the week, do a review. Yes, just like an annual review at work!

Ask yourself:

- How well did I stick to this? Did I do it every day? If not, how many times did I do it this week?
- How did it make me feel? How was this different from how I felt before?
- What were the benefits of doing things this way?

- What could be improved?
- What habits would I like to add to my routine this week?

You'll find this review exercise laid out for you in your Workbook.

ROUTINES OVERWHELM YOU

Our ADHD tendency towards perfection can make routines fail.[2] We dive right in with big ambitions, not realizing we're setting ourselves up for failure. When our attempt at a new habit goes wrong, we blame ourselves for "failing." We struggle to try again because it didn't work for us before, so we think we will only fail again.

You can get past this by:

- Understanding your habits don't have to be perfect. You don't have to fix everything at once. Starting small with that one thing will make it much easier for you to see the benefits. You can then build on it, tailoring whatever you decide to work with your brain instead of trying to force it to fit unrealistic expectations.

- Thinking even smaller. Remember how I said to you to pick one thing you wanted to start with? I bet you chose something ambitious, like cleaning and organizing your bedroom. Break that down even more. Instead of saying, "I'm going to make sure my room is clean and tidy before bed," think smaller. What **one** thing will help make your room neater or more organized? Try, "I'm going to put my dirty clothes in the laundry basket instead of the floor."

> Keeping your floor clear of laundry will have a big impact. That one little win will encourage you to add more *without* feeling overwhelmed.

- Remembering you don't have to do your routine every day. If you really don't want to do something that day, don't! Following your routine 4-5 days a week will still bring you progress.

- Considering what works for you and forgetting everyone else. Everything in this book is just a suggestion. If something makes more sense to you, go for it! If having a shower at night will save you time in the morning, do it. If you want to sleep in your clothes so you don't have to get dressed in the morning, experiment!

What is the one little thing you're going to start with? You'll find space in your Workbook to practice breaking up a big task so you can take one step forward right now.

YOU JUST CAN'T GET MOTIVATED

Reading about how important routines are might make intellectual sense. It doesn't mean you'll be inspired enough to actually follow them. ADHD women often have so many wonderful intentions that we don't act on. And that's perfectly fine.

ADHD brains tend to prioritize the present. The future can feel too distant for us to do something about.[3] But to find the motivation to establish a routine you can:

- Consider yourself in the future. How will you feel in a month if you do everything you set out to do? Who will you become in six months? A year?

  In your Workbook you'll find space to write a letter from your future self discussing what's happened because you were successful in treating and overcoming the challenges of ADHD. In your letter, you will thank yourself for making changes and establishing a routine. This process is incredibly motivating.

- Set up consequences. What could you do for yourself if you got up early every day for work? You might like to treat yourself to an extra long stay in bed on Saturday. Conversely, if you don't follow your routine, you might like to set an alarm on that Saturday so you don't enjoy that lie-in.

- Get other people involved. Find someone you know who can support you as your cheerleader and remind you about your commitment to yourself. I find that a reminder from someone else is more powerful than trying to remind myself. You might like to discuss your habits with them. They might suggest improvements you wouldn't have thought about.

If you found all this sounded good but you'll get to it tomorrow, you've been hit by procrastination. Don't worry. I've got you covered. Turn to the next chapter to see what you can do to beat it.

15

PROCRASTINATION TO ACTION

Motivation Techniques That Work

"Procrastination is like a credit card: it's a lot of fun until you get the bill."

– Christopher Parker

Glancing up at the clock, a surge of adrenaline rushed through me. Turning back to the keyboard, I typed frantically, desperate to complete my assignment before I had to go to class and hand it in. Gulping down what felt like my hundredth coffee, I hit the button to print out my essay, grabbing it just as the alarm I'd set for myself went off to tell me it was time for class.

Rushing down from my dormitory, I managed to make it through the door – just – before collapsing into my seat. I had to stifle a yawn as Professor Findlay collected up the papers. Hopefully that last coffee would help me stay awake for the class. It wouldn't be the first time I'd had to stay up all night to meet a deadline. It probably wouldn't be the last.

Why did I always procrastinate so much?

Well, now I know it was because of my ADHD. While most people procrastinate at some point, for those with ADHD, procrastination is a familiar, unwelcome companion - and it's got its roots in science.

It starts when we're kids. There are some structures in the brains of children with ADHD that are smaller than they would be in a neurotypical child. As we grow, our ADHD brains mature later than neurotypical brains, which is why we don't just 'grow out of' our ADHD.

In the case of procrastination, the issue is with our frontal lobe, which is at the front of the brain, just behind the forehead. This is the part of the brain that deals with decision-making, organization, and impulse control, amongst other things[1].

And that's not all. Studies have also shown that not only are our brains wired differently, but we also have at least one irregular gene. The DRD2 gene makes it harder for our neurons to react to dopamine, the neurotransmitter that helps us feel good and pay attention when we need[2]. This means we may not get the same powerful sense of accomplishment and motivation that helps others push through procrastination. We struggle to comprehend long-term consequences. Immediate gratification? We'd much rather chase that than waste our time on something that may or may not pay off in the long run.

There are emotional factors at play as well:

- Many women with ADHD suffer from anxiety, giving them self-doubt and a fear of failure. This leads to putting things off because it's easier to not do something than to try and fail[3].

- Perfectionism often plagues women with ADHD. When something has to be perfect, or you won't do it, tasks can become insurmountable. You overthink things, trying to get them right, delaying the start[4].

- Problems with focusing is a classic ADHD trait that makes it difficult to do what you're supposed to do when there are so many distractions everywhere. There's a reason why the chapters in this book are short. Any longer, and you'll probably find your mind wandering off![5]

- If you're on the hyperactive end of ADHD, as we've seen earlier in this book, that sense of restlessness makes it challenging to stick with anything for long, so you put things off.

- Women with ADHD often find it hard to get motivated, which makes it almost impossible to get started on something, especially if there isn't an obvious benefit[6].

While I still find it easy to fall prey to procrastination, there are a few strategies I've put in place that make it easier for me to stay on task:

CUT DOWN ON THE NUMBER OF DECISIONS YOU HAVE TO MAKE

Every decision you make takes energy. The more you have to think about choosing what to do, the more energy you spend thinking about it and then end up with nothing left to actually do anything. What should I wear today? What should I have for lunch? Should I check my emails? Should I go to the gym or work on that presentation?

These kinds of questions come up all day long. Those questions need answers. Those answers need decisions. And making decisions all the time is *exhausting*! It's what's known as decision fatigue.[7] Being worn out leads to procrastination. How can you be expected to do anything when you're worn out?

This is why we've gone through planning out your day and scheduling your tasks. Doing this removes a lot of the decision-making regarding what you need to do and when. It cuts back on procrastination because you've already made the choice about what to do and when.

But can you take this even further?

In your Workbook, list out the situations when you find yourself procrastinating. When you've finished, consider whether you can cut back on procrastination by taking even more guesswork out of the equation. For example:

- Do you know what days this week you'll be going to the gym? (Or going out with friends or doing any other activity you enjoy but regularly put off?)
- Do you know what you're going to wear every day?
- Do you know the most important task for tomorrow?

If you don't have the answer to those questions, now is a great time to figure out your replies. Make those decisions **now.** It'll save you so much time in the future. Follow the prompts in your Workbook to help you.

If you haven't been using your Daily Checklist, now you have another incentive to get started. It makes such a difference in removing the overwhelm that comes from having too much to do. You'll find everything you need to set up your Checklist in Chapter Five.

MAKE IT ALL OR NOTHING

This is a strategy I got after reading an article about author Raymond Chandler. He found it hard to sit down and just write until he hit his daily word count. So, he gave himself four hours in the morning to either write or do nothing. Literally nothing.

So, if you've got a job to do and you really don't want to do it when you've scheduled it, that's fine. Don't do the job. But don't do anything else. Don't check your phone. Don't scroll through social media. Don't read a book. Don't watch a video. Don't browse shopping sites. Do literally nothing.

With only two options – do the task or do nothing – eventually, you'll start on the task, if only because it's better than being bored.

So, look at your Master To-Do List. (Because you've made one by now, right?)

What is the most important task on the list?

Schedule 90 minutes in the morning to focus on that task and nothing else. That means no surfing the net. Not doing anything that seems more fun. If you have to put your phone on airplane mode and switch off your wifi, do it.

It's all or nothing.

DO ONE THING AND THEN THE NEXT

Fight the overwhelm that triggers distraction by figuring out the next thing you need to do—not the details, not the overall big picture, but the one little step you need to take to move forward.

Shifting your focus from a huge task to a small one gives you something achievable to do. When you know you can do something easily, you have more energy to do it and feel more motivated. Consequently, you procrastinate less.

Let's say you've got a big PowerPoint presentation to put together for work. Rather than thinking about the enormity of the task, what's one thing you could do right now that would help you make progress?

So, you could choose the layout theme for PowerPoint. It's a small job, but something you can achieve right now. Look! You've made progress. The next small job could be to find the images for the presentation. That won't take long, and suddenly, you're even further along. It won't be long before you find you've finished the project, minus the usual procrastination because you didn't feel like you were climbing an enormous mountain. You were simply stepping over a series of molehills.

One highly effective way to tackle procrastination is to create an environment free from distractions. After all, if you're tackling an addiction, you want to remove the source of temptation. Same with distractions.

In the next chapter, we'll examine how to do that and how to cope when you can't get rid of everything.

16

FOCUSED AND FLOURISHING

Harnessing Concentration On Demand

"Distracted from distraction by distraction."

– T.S. Eliot

"Can you review this report and have it back on my desk by lunchtime?" asked my boss.

"Sure thing."

I settled down to start working through the report to flag any errors. A couple of sentences in, my phone beeped. Picking it up, I saw a text from my friend about going out later that week. Immediately, I tapped out a reply.

Once I was done, I decided to get myself a coffee.

"Could you get me one?" asked Tina in the next cubicle, seeing me get up.

"No problem."

At the coffee machine, I got into a great conversation with Max, a rather good-looking guy who was new to the marketing team. By the time I returned with the coffees, half an hour had passed.

Sweeping aside the papers that had accumulated on my desk, I switched my computer on from sleep mode and started scrolling through emails, adding requested meetings to my calendar and making a note of new jobs that I'd been asked to do. Once that was done, I opened up the presentation I'd been working on. Before I knew it, it was time for lunch.

"Where's that report?" my boss asked as I walked past his office to go grab a bite.

I could have kicked myself. The *report!* If only I hadn't been distracted…

It used to happen to me all the time. I'd start one job only to get sidetracked into doing something else and then something else. It seemed like I couldn't do anything from start to finish without something else grabbing my attention.

I didn't understand why I couldn't stay focused until I found the explanation thanks to scientific research. It turns out that women with ADHD are usually highly sensitive, which means that our brains get caught up in processing external stimuli, regardless of whether it's relevant to the task at hand or not. This makes us more likely to get distracted as our mind wanders off, or we get bombarded with intrusive thoughts. Problems with our processing systems mean it's harder for us to force our minds to stay on topic because we're compelled to follow those distracting thoughts through to the end, so our minds end up a long way from whatever it is we're supposed to be thinking about[1]. That's why it's so important to eliminate distractions as much as possible. Here's what's worked for me to stop myself from being distracted. If you introduce just one of these recommendations, you'll find you're less distracted, too.

DITCH YOUR PHONE AND TELEVISION

Staying away from your phone or television while you work (or perform any other important task) will help you focus on the job at hand.

Having the TV playing while you're trying to do something is a distraction. The moment something interesting comes on, there's a chance you'll stop what you should be doing to watch that instead. It's the same with having videos playing on your phone.

Women with ADHD often suffer from object permanence. This means quite literally, if it's out of sight, it's out of mind[2].

Put your TV in storage for a week and see if you miss it. Chances are you won't. Put your phone in a different room while you're trying to get something done. You'll find that the fewer distractions around, the less you'll be distracted.

SWITCH OFF INTERNET ACCESS

Even if you didn't have ADHD, it's easy to find yourself down a rabbit hole when something grabs your interest. Make it impossible for this to happen by switching off your wifi box, turning off mobile data on your phone, and, if you can, going somewhere with no internet access while you work.

Even if you can't be completely internet-free, you can at least close all the apps on your device that need the internet so you can work offline for a while.

Pro tip: When you're creating your Checklist, separate out tasks that need internet access. Give yourself internet-free time when you're doing something that isn't reliant on the internet. For example, if you have research that needs to be done online for a project, once it's done, save the information and work with it offline. You'll find it easier to finish the project without the distraction of being online.

SWITCH OFF NOTIFICATIONS

There's no need to have push notifications enabled on all your apps. Much as you might love knowing that someone's sent you an email, chances are it doesn't need your attention right away.

Set up times for checking email and other notifications. Outside those scheduled times, don't worry about missing out. Now you've got a regular schedule for staying in contact, you'll never miss out on anything. I promise you that the world won't end if you go half an hour without getting a notification.

SET UP A QUIET PLACE

If you have a place you can go to focus, it can often help you avoid distractions. This could be a local coffee shop, a library, the park, or a room set aside in your home or office—anywhere relatively minimalist and doesn't have the distractions associated with your usual workplace. You may need to experiment to find quieter times to go to a coffee shop; otherwise, you might find yourself getting distracted by others.

Mix things up as well. Some days, it's nice to work by a pond or lake with ducks swimming about. Other times, being in the library helps to get into a work mindset.

Schedule regular times in the week to go to your quiet place to focus on your most important jobs without being distracted.

CLEAN UP

Clutter, clutter, clutter! If necessary, go back to Chapter 13 to organize your space and remove the clutter. Use the Workbook Exercise 18 – Get Organized – again if you have to! The fewer things you have floating around you, the less there is to distract you with the need to fiddle or tidy.

ONLY HAVE ONE WINDOW OPEN AT A TIME ON YOUR COMPUTER

It's very easy to end up having a ton of browser tabs and apps open all over your computer. This digital clutter is just as much of a distraction as a messy desk and noisy environment.

Stop trying to multitask. Single-task instead. Having lots of windows open makes it hard to find what you need and prevents you from focusing on the job at hand.

If you're going through your email, close all other windows and only read your emails. If you're doing some internet research, close all browsers except one and focus on that.

I'll admit that it does take some practice to get into the habit of having one thing open at a time, but it really does make it easier to concentrate.

NO IS A COMPLETE SENTENCE

The simplest way to prevent distractions is to know when to say no. Say no when you're asked to join a meeting at short notice.

When you start saying no to things instead of yes to everything, your productivity shoots up as if by magic.

Say no to that project being dumped on you at the last minute. Say no to answering when someone calls at an inconvenient time and let it go to voicemail.

Resist the urge to be a people pleaser and to try getting all the things done. You've done that before, and if it worked out for you the same as it did for me, you need a new approach.

Instead, stop overloading yourself and start using the word "no" more often. Look at your calendar and see whether you really do have time for that extra job. Get familiar with your daily schedule and know what room you have for anything extra. If there's no room, then pull out your power word: "no!"

When you start saying no to things instead of yes to everything, your productivity shoots up as if by magic.

This section of the book has covered a lot of information on improving productivity through helpful habits, routines and organization so you can reach your goals and maximize your potential. Now, it's time to move on to the other areas of life and see how you can achieve your personal goals, too.

PART 4

Thriving in Life and Relationships

17

OPTIMIZING YOUR WELLNESS

Holistic Approaches To ADHD Health

"If we have been judged for the parts of us that show up as ADHD, eating disorders, or trauma responses, it makes sense that there might be a part who is vigilant about being rejected. Instead of judging this part, perhaps we can get to know it better and offer care and understanding."

– Dr. Sand Chang

> *My husband and I watched in stunned amazement at the tantrum my daughter was throwing. It was weird because she wasn't angry. She wasn't frustrated. She was just so filled with energy that a tantrum was the only way she could work it off – and all from one little sweet.*
>
> *My sister had brought a bag of pineapple-flavored sweets back from her trip to New Zealand for us to try and we'd given one to Tiana. Almost as soon as she put it in her mouth, she was a different child, quite literally bouncing off the walls. We didn't dare give her another one!*
>
> *We'd noticed that she was sensitive to some food additives and colorings, but this was something else. It was a real eye-opener about how important it was to give good food to my daughter with ADHD to help manage her behavior. – Elise M.*

Evidence suggests that diet plays some part in how ADHD affects you[1]. It's the principle of garbage in, garbage out at play – eat nutrient-rich food and your symptoms are more easily controlled. Eat junk food high in sugar, artificial flavors, and allergens, and your symptoms can take over your life. That doesn't mean you can't ever enjoy another chocolate bar, but once you know the effect it has on you, you may well find yourself choosing a piece of fruit instead.

The good news is that there isn't a specific ADHD diet that requires hours of research followed by hours of preparation in the kitchen.

It's straightforward. Try to make sure that every meal consists of half fruits or vegetables, a quarter protein, and a quarter carbohydrates.

In fact, you probably already know what constitutes a healthy diet but may not have realized how important it is for your ADHD symptoms. But just in case you don't know what to choose, here's a quick rundown of foods to eat to support optimal brain function.

PROTEIN

Protein-rich foods can support your ADHD brain to be more effective[2]. Protein can be found in lean, unprocessed meat, poultry, fish, eggs, nuts, beans, dairy products, and soy. Protein is utilized by the body to make neurotransmitters, which are the chemicals brain cells use to communicate. It also helps to keep blood sugar in check, preventing those sudden surges that can make you more hyperactive and impulsive.

Make sure you have good sources of protein with your breakfast, such as poached eggs or yogurt sprinkled with nuts. Then, if you can, have protein throughout the day. Try keeping some protein bars in your purse for when you need a snack or taking a protein-filled smoothie with you to work to sip on.

COMPLEX CARBOHYDRATES

Carbs have received rough treatment, with diets such as Atkins advocating cutting them out completely. However, carbs are important for brain function and mood regulation.[3]

Look for foods with what's called a low glycemic index (GI). Foods with a high GI encourage the pancreas to generate high doses of insulin, causing a sugar rush that leaves a slump when it wears off. Low GI foods provide a steadier source of blood sugar, helping you to manage your symptoms.[4]

Fruits such as grapefruit, apples, oranges, cherries, and grapes are a good source of carbohydrates, although check with your clinician that they don't affect any medications you may be on. Fruits in their raw form have a lower GI than fruit juices because they contain fiber, which slows the body's absorption of sugar.

Cereals and grains such as oatmeal, bran, wholemeal cereals, and pasta have comparatively low GIs. Try to avoid more sugary cereals, such as cornflakes and processed breakfast cereals. Since dairy products also have low GIs, you can combine these with cereals for a healthy breakfast. Try oatmeal with blueberries or plain yogurt with sliced apple.

Legumes, including kidney beans and lentils, have some of the lowest GI of all foods. Vegetables such as potatoes and sweet potatoes are also good sources of carbohydrates.

VITAMINS AND MINERALS

Even with a healthy diet, you may benefit from extra supplements to ensure you have all the vitamins and minerals you need. Taking supplements daily with any other medications you may be on will ensure you get those essential nutrients, even on days when you forget to eat regularly.

Ones which are particularly valuable for women with ADHD include:

- Zinc, iron, and magnesium. Zinc and iron are essential for producing dopamine, a neurotransmitter that helps you stay motivated. People with ADHD tend to be low in dopamine, which explains the problems with inattention. Magnesium also creates neurotransmitters known to be associated with focus, as well as having a calming effect. While you can find these minerals in lean meat, poultry, seafood, soy, nuts, and fortified cereals, you may want to supplement them to raise your mineral levels.[5]

- B vitamins. Vitamin B-6, in particular, has been identified as boosting dopamine levels[6]. You can get it in your diet from fish, beef liver, starchy vegetables such as potatoes, and non-citrus fruit.

- Omega-3 fatty acids. There is plenty of evidence supporting the benefit of omega-3s for people with ADHD[7]. However, since it's predominantly found in oily fish like sardines, salmon, and tuna, if you're not eating plenty of fish, you won't be getting enough omega-3. Go for a high-quality supplement – it's worth the investment.

- Gingko and ginseng. Studies have shown that these herbs reduce impulsivity and distractedness[8]. They act like stimulants on the brain in much the same way as ADHD medication but don't have the same side effects. If you're hesitant to try medication, these herbs would be a good alternative to try.

FOODS TO AVOID

As well as eating healthy, nutrient dense foods, it's important to cut out foods known to be a trigger for ADHD symptoms. If you're not sure whether a particular food is a trigger for you, try keeping a food diary for a couple of weeks, noting how you were feeling before and after you ate. There's a worksheet you can use for this in your Workbook. You'll soon notice any patterns to identify problem foods for you.

Sugar

As a general rule, avoid foods and snacks high in sugar. Check food labels to see whether they contain substances such as high-fructose corn sweetener, dehydrated cane juice, dextrose, sucrose, dextrin, maltodextrin, molasses, malt syrup, or molasses. These are all red flags. While the evidence is mixed as to whether sugar negatively impacts those with ADHD, there's plenty of anecdotal evidence to support sugary foods exacerbating ADHD symptoms[9].

Artificial colorings and additives

While we tend to think of children as the ones most affected by artificial additives, it can still be an issue for adults. We simply learn how to hide our behaviors a little more effectively as we get older[10]. Avoid anything brightly colored. If it doesn't occur in nature, don't put it in your mouth!

Allergens

It is worth getting yourself checked for food allergies because these could be making your ADHD symptoms worse. Your reactions may not have been physical in nature, which is why you can be allergic to a food and not realize it. Again, food diaries can help identify whether an allergy is affecting your brain function.

Foods that commonly cause issues with ADHD include milk, wheat, corn, and soy.[11]

While it can feel overwhelming to radically overhaul your diet, as you start eating foods that support your ADHD brain, not only will you feel better, you'll find you enjoy your meals more because you're fueling your body with what it really craves.

In your Workbook, you'll find a suggested menu for a typical day. You'll see that meals can be easy – and affordable – to make from scratch. It's a simple way of reducing the impact of ADHD on your life. Pick a dish from that menu to make for today, or use it to inspire another similar meal you'd really enjoy.

If you're still struggling to improve your diet, it's worth enlisting the help of a friend. However, many women with ADHD find it challenging to build and keep friendships. That's why we will look at what you can do to build a social circle in the next chapter.

18

BUILDING YOUR SOCIAL CIRCLE

Friendship Strategies
For Women With ADHD

"After a gap in communication, some women with ADHD become ashamed and let the friendship slip away rather than try to explain their silence."

– Ellen Littman

When I saw the notice go up about a new book club at work, my heart sank.

I always felt like an outcast in the office. Other people at work would go out for drinks and seem like best buddies while I didn't have a clue how to get asked to go along. I knew book clubs were supposed to be good places to make friends. If no one asked if I wanted to join, I'd feel like no one cared. But if I did get invited, they'd quickly discover I hated reading!

I guess I was doomed to spend my life alone...
– Samantha D.

Friendships can be hard when you have ADHD. They're built on mutual understanding, cooperation, emotional availability, and making the effort to stay friends. They require a high degree of executive function, which can make it challenging for women with ADHD to keep up.

What people don't tend to mention is that friendships also require energy. Another resource that women with ADHD don't always have in abundance. It's enough just trying to get through the day. We need downtime to recover from the mental exertion that ADHD can demand. Spending time alone is a joy because we don't have to maintain a pretense of functioning like others. Yet we're desperate to build those connections with others, which makes us promise more than we can deliver because, just like others, we want to be accepted.

Turn on the TV and you'll be bombarded with shows filled with groups of women all happily hanging out, supporting each other, spending time together, and enjoying friendships. It feels like everyone else gets to have a gang of friends except us. This perceived contrast can be detrimental to our health.

According to a report released by the Surgeon General of the United States, loneliness is as damaging to our wellbeing as smoking[1].

There are two types of ADHD friends. Which one are you?

If you have hyperactive/impulsive ADHD, you will:

- Butt in during conversations and try to dominate
- Get bored easily
- Ignore social conventions
- Say what's on your mind, no matter how negative
- Talk about yourself too much
- Use alcohol in social situations
- Walk away from frustrating relationships

If you have inattentive ADHD, you will:

- Find emotional demands overwhelming
- Feel anxious in unfamiliar social settings
- Self-censor to avoid conflict

- Avoid unstructured group situations
- Retreat inwardly when you feel overstimulated
- Blame yourself for social mistakes
- Expect you'll be criticized or rejected

When we have managed to make friends, ADHD women can be the best friends you could ever want – when we're actively spending time together. But the moment a friend goes home, we lose the enthusiasm and passion we felt for being with them. It's not that we don't want to care. We do. But object permanence is, once again, at odds with us.

If someone isn't there, no matter how much we value them, they drop off our radar to make room for more pressing matters. When something happens to remind us that they exist, we remember how much we love our friends, but then we worry that it's been so long that they've either forgotten about us or given up on us because they're offended that we haven't been bothering.

Our emotional dysregulation can lead to rejection sensitivity, so we avoid situations that might make us feel as though we're disliked or unwanted. This leads to us saying no to invitations and deciding not to go to events because we'd rather stay home and feel lonely than go out and have people make us feel bad for being ourselves[2].

Friendships require maintenance, regular notes to say, "How are things?" to show you care. We know we do, but other people often assume we're not interested anymore because they haven't heard from us in a while. The longer it goes without a message, the harder it becomes to reach out. It's embarrassing when you've left it too long. We feel ashamed for not being a good friend. So, we let the friendship go instead of trying to make it up to them.

However, as awareness grows around ADHD and more people open up about the effect it has on them, the more options there are to help you keep those friends who mean so much.

USE TECHNOLOGY

Just because friendships rely on regular communication, that doesn't mean you have to spend hours staying in touch with everyone. Make things easier for yourself by using technology to support your friendships.

- Send a quick text or private message on social media. Just a quick "thinking of you" can mean a lot and put a smile on a friend's face.
- Use reminders to keep track of important dates like birthdays.

TELL YOUR FRIENDS ABOUT YOUR ADHD

People are a lot more understanding when they know there's a reason for your behavior. Let your friends know that you may not be great at quick replies to texts and emails, but their messages are important, and you'll do your best to get back to them as soon as you can.

If you find that a friendship is making you feel stressed and guilty more than it makes you happy, you may want to consider whether it's right for you to keep that friendship. It's not worth spending precious energy trying to convince someone that your ADHD is behind the problems and you're doing your best when they don't believe ADHD is a problem - or don't believe you have it in the first place. If they don't want to understand, they never will, no matter how hard you try. Remember, there are lots of people out there who are more open-minded and accepting of someone that is dealing with the challenges of ADHD.

UNDERSTAND YOUR TRIGGERS

As you've worked through this book, you'll have learned a lot about what exacerbates your ADHD symptoms. Our ADHD brains are on a constant lookout for stimulation, which can make us interrupt conversations with unrelated comments, change the subject, or zone out.

Although women with ADHD may share many similarities, what makes us tick will be unique. We might both have triggers, but mine will be different from yours. Knowing your triggers will help you manage them, making for much more satisfying relationships. In your Workbook, you'll find an exercise to help you recognize your triggers and find solutions for managing them.

Make it easier for yourself to focus on your friends. If you've gone out for drinks or dinner, try to sit in the middle so you've got people talking on either side. That way, if you find yourself losing interest in one conversation, you can switch to the one going on on your other side.

If you find yourself getting restless or fidgety, don't try to push through it. Instead, go to the restroom to give yourself a break to refresh. Have a quick walk around the building. Spend a few minutes checking your phone. Do something so your brain gets to recharge. Then, if you still think you're going to feel restless, give yourself a reason to leave early and don't feel ashamed for going. You're honoring your needs. Your friends will, too.

BE THERE

A major part of being a good friend is simply being there. Whenever you have an opportunity to meet up with others, take it, even if you don't feel in the mood. The more time you spend with someone, the stronger your friendship becomes. Even if you don't stay long, the effort will be appreciated.

BECOME PART OF A GROUP

Find a club or activity that interests you and join in. It's the easiest way to make new friends. You've got an automatic topic of conversation you know everyone enjoys. You get to meet lots of people at once, which can make it easier to build friendships because you gain plenty of friends at the same time rather than having to work on each person individually. This is an added bonus if you're struggling to find time for friendships.

If you can't find a group that suits you, set one up. You may be surprised at who comes. You're probably not the only one who was waiting for a club to talk about movies or wine tasting.

The LearnWell Community is a great choice too.

GIVE YOURSELF A GOAL

While we think friendships develop organically, there's a lot you can do to grow your social circle. For example, whenever you're going into a situation where you'll meet new people, set yourself a target of making two new friends. When you go in with the intention of being friendly, you may well find it makes you feel more open to building connections and make an effort to go into more depth than a smattering of small talk.

And smile! Smiling makes you appear friendlier, making people want to be friends with you.

Remember to use the strategies discussed earlier in the book as well. Techniques such as DEARMAN can help you maintain friendships and work through any issues that may arise.

I want to explore a little deeper how ADHD affects our relationships. Specifically, we'll examine romantic relationships and how you can ensure that your ADHD doesn't sabotage your efforts to find and maintain love.

19

LOVE AND ADHD

Nurturing Healthy Partnerships

"Marrying the right person and finding the right job are probably the two most important 'treatments' for adults."

– Edward M. Hallowell

 I've written this chapter for those seeking new relationships. For those of you with established relationships already, you may choose to skip this chapter.

I never thought I'd find that 'happy ever after' I dreamed about. I bounced from one relationship to another and there was always one problem: me.

I was too much, too demanding, too quirky, too flakey, too... too... too...

My ADHD diagnosis helped me understand that I wasn't a problem at all. Yes, my ADHD could make dating complicated, but that didn't make me unlovable.

Building healthy, loving relationships when you have ADHD can be tricky. That's why you might want to read the book: "ADHD Tools For Couples." It was also published by LearnWell Books and covers how ADHD can complicate relationships, including the research that shows that we're navigating problems other people don't have to consider. Love isn't always enough when one or both partners are neurodivergent. ADHD Tools For Couples is filled with strategies and techniques to help you work together to build a strong relationship.

Here are some of the tips I've found useful for navigating new relationships in the early stages.

MAKE A LIST

Women with ADHD often experience emotions with heightened intensity. This emotional sensitivity can be both a strength and a challenge, particularly in romantic relationships. When we feel a strong connection with someone, it's easy for our emotions to take the lead, sometimes overshadowing logical considerations.

To navigate this, it can be helpful to create a thoughtful framework for evaluating potential partners. In your Workbook, you'll find an exercise to create a "Partner Qualities List." This isn't about creating unrealistic expectations but rather about identifying values and traits that align with your needs and lifestyle.

When creating your list, focus on positive attributes. For example, instead of "Doesn't get frustrated with my forgetfulness," you might write "Is patient and understanding." Consider including ADHD-specific traits that are important to you, such as "Appreciates neurodiversity" or "Supports my ADHD management strategies."

From experience, the two most important qualities on my list are patience and understanding. You're building a partnership that could potentially go on to last a lifetime. Even with a solid foundation of knowing about your ADHD and accepting it, there will be times when something unexpected happens, or your symptoms are worse than usual. Being with someone who can be patient when you're going through a rough time and understand that it's not deliberate and you're trying your best makes a world of difference.

The Workbook provides prompts and examples to help you get started, but remember that this list should reflect your unique preferences and needs. It's a living document – feel free to revisit and revise it as you learn more about yourself and your relationship needs.

Once completed, this list can serve as a helpful reference when you're getting to know someone new. It's not about finding a perfect match for every item but rather about assessing overall compatibility and ensuring your core needs are met. This approach can help balance emotional excitement with practical considerations, leading to more fulfilling relationships.

Remember, while this list is a useful tool, it's equally important to remain open to unexpected connections and to trust your instincts. The goal is to find a balance between heart and mind, embracing the emotional richness that comes with ADHD while making informed choices about your relationships.

TAKE THINGS SLOW

Our ADHD brains love the hit of dopamine that comes from a whirlwind relationship. We tend to fall hard and fast, but then that rush wears off, and we end what could have been something beautiful if we'd taken the time to let things develop.

Knowing the ADHD tendency to be impulsive and rush into things can help you slow down when you notice yourself abandoning sensible controls. Refer back to your list to remind yourself of what you're looking for in a partner. It's worth noting that individuals with ADHD may be at higher risk for sexually transmitted infections due to tendencies toward impulsivity and risk-taking behaviors.[1] When starting a new relationship, it can be beneficial to take things slowly and ensure there's a genuine connection beyond initial attraction. Practicing safe sex and open communication about sexual health is important for everyone but may require extra mindfulness for those managing ADHD symptoms.

BE HONEST RIGHT FROM THE START

You probably already know the habits that have caused issues in your previous relationships. You'll have been told about them over and over. While reading this book shows how hard you're working to deal with your ADHD symptoms, there will still be times when they still cause problems.

Consider being upfront about your communication style early on. For example, you might say, "I get really enthusiastic in conversations and sometimes jump in quickly. I'm working on it, but please let me know if I interrupt." This kind of openness can foster understanding and set the stage for better communication. It also shows self-awareness and a willingness to grow. Likewise, if you have other traits and quirks that you know have been problematic in past relationships, think about how you might frame them so your date can get to know you better and understand a little more about why you do what you do.

You don't need to disclose your ADHD if you're not comfortable with it, but discussing your traits can lead to more meaningful interactions and mutual respect. Plus, acknowledging these tendencies often helps you manage them better.

DON'T TAKE IT PERSONALLY

Navigating romantic relationships can be challenging for everyone, and some individuals with ADHD may experience heightened emotional sensitivity. Research suggests that rejection sensitive dysphoria (RSD) can be more common among people with ADHD, though it's not exclusive to ADHD and doesn't affect everyone with the condition equally.[2]

If you find yourself feeling particularly hurt by perceived rejection, it can be helpful to remember that other people's actions are often more about their own circumstances than a reflection on you. In dating, lack of compatibility doesn't equate to personal failure.

When faced with unclear communication or "ghosting," it's natural to feel frustrated or confused. It's also worth bearing in mind that when you have ADHD, you can be equally guilty of ghosting! If a message comes in from a date, you may mean to reply but get distracted so don't get back to it for hours, days, or even over a week. Or, you may find that you're unsure what to say when replying so don't say anything at all, or feel overwhelmed by having a conversation at that moment.

Ultimately, the key to any successful relationship is communication. Just as you might not be replying to a text or message because you're feeling stressed or overwhelmed, your date or boyfriend might be having similar feelings too. If they're not responding to a message, it could be more to do with how they're feeling and nothing to do with how much they care about you.

Be open about how you're feeling. Ask your partner to be more mindful in making sure they get back to you when you need and listen if they need you to work on your communication a little more. Talk about what's going on, why, and what strategies you might be able to put in place to improve your communication. There are lots of helpful tips in this book and "ADHD Tools for Couples" you can draw upon for inspiration.

A suggestion a friend of mine made when I was telling her how hard it was for me to deal with texting to arrange a date was to get a low-light telescope for smartphones. It sounds weird but it really works! I was getting distracted by notifications and checking out social media whenever I needed to send a text. Using a low-light telescope cut back how much stimulation I got from the screen so I could concentrate better on just sending a text. It wasn't a miracle cure, but it definitely improved my ability to text someone to arrange a get-together.

STAY SAFE

While the desire to make a good impression is common in dating, it's important for everyone to prioritize their safety and comfort. This advice applies regardless of neurodiversity, but when you have ADHD, you're more prone to being impulsive and putting yourself in risky situations for the dopamine rush.

For early dates, meeting in public places is generally recommended. This allows you to get to know someone in a safe environment. Trust your instincts - if you feel uncomfortable for any reason, it's okay to end the date early. Having a pre-arranged check-in with a friend can be a helpful safety measure for anyone.

When using online dating platforms, it's wise to be cautious. According to a Pew Research Center study[3], about 71% of online daters believe it's common for people to lie to appear more desirable. If you notice significant discrepancies between someone's online profile and their in-person presentation, it's okay to be wary.

Remember, prioritizing your safety isn't rude - it's a form of self-care.

KEEP YOUR EYES OPEN FOR RED FLAGS

When dating, it's important for everyone to be aware of their personal boundaries and comfort levels. While getting to know someone involves sharing personal information, this typically happens gradually as trust builds.

The problem is that when you have ADHD, taking things slow isn't always easy. Our brain chemistry means that a new romantic relationship gives our oxytocin and dopamine a massive hit, so it's almost like we're addicted to our new love interest.

I remember one guy I met on a dating app. We spent about ten minutes messaging and then I asked him if he fancied meeting up. Later that afternoon, we were talking over a few drinks. Or rather, I was the one doing most of the talking, as I told him all about previous dates, my life history, and my career ambitions. There was a little voice inside me that was whispering at me to take things slow, but I couldn't seem to help myself. We agreed to meet up again, and it wasn't long before I found myself thinking about him all the time - right up until the point he broke up with me a few months later because I was moving too fast and he wasn't ready for a serious relationship. I didn't think it was that serious - I was just having fun!

However, what *is* serious is the fact that having ADHD puts you at greater risk of abuse in a relationship.[4] Our ADHD susceptibility to intense love and deep attractions makes us more open to being manipulated, say when a potential partner is love-bombing us. Our impulsive nature makes it hard to maintain healthy boundaries if a partner starts to be controlling. For example, they might claim that our problems with financial matters mean that they should take over handling the money for our own good when really it's an excuse to control us. (And we're more than capable of dealing with our finances once we've been equipped with the right tools.) Our ADHD brains struggle with attention, memory, staying organized, etc. can all be used to gaslight us and make us question whether we're doing something wrong.

When you made your list of what you want from a romantic partner, you will have included things that were red flags for you. If you want to avoid someone who is controlling, look for someone who is happy for you to have your freedom and accepts you for who you are. If you don't want to be gaslit, look for someone who validates you rather than makes you second guess yourself.

And **don't** ignore these red flags because you're loving the dopamine you're getting from someone!

There are plenty of women with ADHD who are in successful, loving relationships. Of course, this can be with someone who also has ADHD or another form of neurodiversity. People whose brains have similar wiring to ours understand what we're going through because they've had similar experiences.

You don't need to put up with being criticized or devalued by a partner. You can decide what an ideal relationship would look like for you and choose not to accept anything else. In this book, you've been given a lot of tools for understanding your ADHD and how it affects you. You can build on these to see how they show up in your romantic relationships and work on techniques to deal with your symptoms. The more self-aware you are, the more you can be open with your partner so they know what you need from them and what you can and can't do. You might also find it helpful to talk about your relationship with your friends and ask them to help you identify what you're doing that's supportive and what you might need to work on more. (They're also good at helping you see red flags you might not have noticed.)

And always remember to **take things slow.** Take the time to connect with how you're *really* feeling about someone when you're not riding a dopamine high. You might like to journal regularly about how your relationship is making you feel about yourself, what you think and feel about a potential partner, and whether the relationship is working for you. Journaling is another way of identifying red flags. When you understand the signs, you'll feel more confident in walking away when a relationship isn't working for you. Even if they're really, really hot!

BRING UP YOUR ADHD WHEN IT FEELS RIGHT FOR YOU

Your ADHD diagnosis is personal, private medical information. You don't have to tell anyone about it if you don't want to. While you're going to want to share it with your partner at some point, it's up to you when you feel the time is right. Some people like to mention it early when they're dating as a way of eliminating people who aren't going to be understanding in the long term. Others prefer to wait until there's a stronger emotional connection to be able to talk it through and explain the impact ADHD has on them.

Whenever you decide to disclose your diagnosis, how your partner reacts will tell you a lot about them as a person. If they aren't supportive and open to learning more, then they're not the right person for you.

As we've seen, managing our emotions plays a crucial role in our relationships and daily interactions. Our experiences with emotional intensity and impulsivity can significantly impact how we connect with others and navigate various life situations. In the next chapter, we'll explore practical strategies for managing these aspects of ADHD.

20

THE IMPULSE ADVANTAGE

Channeling ADHD Energy Positively

"You don't need to be sorry for being emotional. Your emotions are beautiful."

– Firdous

I feel like I'm always at the whim of my emotions. If my husband asks me – perfectly politely – if I did something, I blow up. It feels like he's keeping tabs on me, making me feel like I'm less than him when all he wants to do is find out if he needs to do it. I yell at my kids if they don't get a good grade or get into trouble at school. I get angry at them when really I'm angry at myself. I was exactly like them and I want them to avoid the problems I had. It's so frustrating to see history repeat itself. – Lori W.

Managing emotions can be a challenge associated with ADHD for some. This may be related to aspects of ADHD, such as differences in executive function and impulse control.

Emotional dysregulation is common in women with ADHD due to our brain wiring. It is the reduced ability to manage and regulate our emotions and consequent reactions. It starts at the amygdala, located in the temporal lobes of the brain just above the ears. When the amygdala gets flooded with a particular emotion, it sends a signal to the cerebral cortex, the outer layer of the brain, which deals with important functions like thinking and emotional responses. In a neurotypical person, the cerebral cortex dampens the instinctive emotional response, so the individual has a chance to pause and consider how they will react. In someone who has ADHD, the connection between the amygdala and cerebral cortex isn't as strong, so our emotions can be all over the place. That's what makes it look like we're overreacting or, conversely, not reacting enough[1].

This can make our behavior seem erratic and our emotional responses over the top. It can manifest in big mood swings (which has led to many women being misdiagnosed with mood disorders), little patience for frustration, sudden bursts of anger, crying, anxiety, and depression. Our positive emotions are also affected – I can literally dance with excitement and happiness!

In addition to the various strategies you've seen in this book already, here are some extra tips to manage your emotions:

REMEMBER THAT EMOTIONS AREN'T A BAD THING

Emotions play a vital role in our lives, serving as natural responses to our experiences and often motivating positive change. They can inspire us to address injustices and make important life decisions. It's crucial to understand that all emotions are valid, and it's okay to feel them fully. However, the challenge lies in managing our reactions to these emotions, especially in ways that don't harm ourselves or others.

When you sense your emotions intensifying, try silently reminding yourself, "I am experiencing these emotions, but they do not define me." Such simple practices can create a moment of pause, allowing you to step back from the immediacy of your feelings.

During this pause, you can use your mindfulness strategies such as deep breathing. These techniques can help you regain a sense of calm and perspective, enabling you to respond to the situation more thoughtfully rather than reacting impulsively. Remember, the goal isn't to suppress your emotions but to navigate them in a way that aligns with your values and long-term well-being.

KNOW YOUR WARNING SIGNS

What happens when your emotions are getting out of control? Are you irritable? Do you get impatient? Do you feel like you explode? Are there any physical signs like a tightening in your chest or clenching your jaw?

Learn your personal early warning signals. You'll find space in your Workbook to list them out. You can then use these to identify times when you fall into old patterns and actively work to do things differently. For example, if you find yourself always arguing with your partner in the evening, wait to talk about difficult subjects until the morning when you're not so tired. When you're worn out, it's harder to stay calm.

TAKE A TIME-OUT

Emotional regulation strategies are valuable tools for adults, especially those managing ADHD symptoms. The concept of a "time-out" can be reframed as a mindful pause or strategic retreat, allowing you to process your emotions more effectively.

When you feel overwhelmed or frustrated, consider implementing a structured break:

- Recognize the need: Be aware of your emotional state and physical cues that signal rising tension.

- Communicate clearly: Express your need for a pause in a calm, assertive manner. For example, "I'm feeling overwhelmed and need some time to gather my thoughts. Can we revisit this in 30 minutes?"

- Use the time productively: During your break, employ calming techniques such as deep breathing, progressive muscle relaxation, or a brief mindfulness exercise. These can help reset your emotional state.

- Reflect and plan: Consider the source of your frustration and brainstorm potential solutions or compromises.

- Re-engage constructively: Return to the discussion with a clearer mind and, if possible, potential resolutions.

Remember, taking time to process your emotions isn't a sign of weakness; it's a mature approach to managing complex feelings and interactions. By doing so, you're more likely to respond thoughtfully rather than react impulsively, potentially avoiding regrettable words or actions.

EXERCISE

Burn off anger and tension with some exercise so you can approach a situation rationally. Go for a walk or run and get some fresh air. It'll help you look at things from a different perspective. Make sure you're eating properly with food that supports your ADHD (Chapter 17) and get a good night's sleep, too.

LISTEN

All too often, we spend our time planning what we want to say when someone is talking instead of listening to what they're telling us. Make a conscious choice to really listen to what the other person is saying. It may not be what you think.

One helpful way to ensure you've truly listened is to paraphrase what they've just told you to check your understanding. That gives the other person the opportunity to correct any misconceptions, which leads to better communication. Use GIVE and the other skills you learned in chapter 10 to help you improve your listening skills.

SLOW DOWN TO FEEL

Some women with ADHD find themselves getting caught in emotional thought loops. We might fixate on something someone said or did, replaying it over and over in our minds. This can lead to a flood of intense feelings that seem impossible to shake off.

When you notice this happening, try to pause and create a moment of mindful awareness. Sit with your emotions without judgment. Ask yourself:

- How does this situation truly make me feel?
- What specific thoughts keep coming up?
- Are these thoughts helping me in any way?
- What might it feel like to release these thoughts?

Remember, the goal isn't to force the thoughts away but to observe them with curiosity. This practice can help create some emotional distance, allowing you to see the situation more clearly.

Your Workbook contains several journaling prompts designed to help you navigate through these intense emotional experiences. Use these prompts to explore your feelings more deeply. Writing can be a powerful tool for processing emotions and gaining new perspectives on challenging situations.

By regularly practicing this kind of emotional awareness, you may find that over time, you can move through intense feelings more easily without getting stuck in repetitive thought patterns.

USE A FIDGET TOY

There's a broad range of fidget toys available for adults. You can even get jewelry to wear so you can fidget without it being obvious. Fidgeting helps you let go of frustration and built-up energy, making it easier for you to use all the strategies you've learned throughout this book.

Emotional regulation may be more difficult when you have ADHD, but it's a skill that can be learned, just like any other. You just have to be willing to do the work. Not everything will work for you, so experiment with the various strategies and be kind to yourself if something isn't a good fit. The right tools are available to support you as you manage your emotions and enjoy more harmonious relationships.

In the next chapter we're going to look at how to reach your goals with techniques that really work.

21

GOAL SETTING FOR THE ADHD MIND

Turning Aspirations Into Achievements

"If you want to live a happy life, tie it to a goal, not people or things."

— Albert Einstein

Do you have life goals? Things you want to achieve that would see you living your dream?

We hear time and again about the importance of goals. Motivational speakers like Tony Robbins and Daymond John will tell you that goals are crucial to success. What we don't hear is that all the powerful goal-setting strategies taught at seminars and by business coaches don't automatically apply to women with ADHD. How we achieve success may need to be reconsidered to accommodate our divergent ways of thinking.

Of course, that doesn't mean we have to give up on our goals. We might just need to consider an alternative approach to achieving them. Luckily, I've discovered a range of strategies that *do* work for us, and I'm going to share them with you now.

WORK WITH YOUR STRENGTHS, NOT YOUR WEAKNESSES

In recent years, there's been a shift in thinking about personal development. Many experts now suggest that focusing solely on improving weaknesses may not be the most effective approach, especially for individuals with ADHD. This perspective is particularly relevant for women with ADHD, many of whom have spent years feeling like they're constantly falling short.

Instead, let's flip that. Identifying and leveraging your unique strengths can be transformative. This doesn't mean ignoring areas for improvement but rather creating a balanced approach that celebrates your talents while finding creative solutions for challenges.

Consider this: successful people often build teams around them to complement their skills. Why not apply the same principle to your life? If numbers make your head spin, collaborating with an accountant could be a smart move. Drowning in administrative tasks? A virtual assistant might be a lifesaver. By delegating tasks that drain your energy, you free up mental space to focus on what you do best.

Your Workbook includes a great exercise to help you identify and appreciate your strengths. It offers prompts to guide you through this process, encouraging you to recognize skills you might have overlooked. Acknowledging your 'superpowers' isn't just a feel-good exercise—it's a strategic approach to personal and professional growth.

If you struggle to know your gifts because your self-esteem has been eroded, here are some strengths that frequently feature in women with ADHD:

- We're frequently more creative than neurotypical people. If you need innovative solutions or suggestions for new ideas, we're the ones to ask.

- We have a lot of empathy, possibly because of how much we've had to go through. This can help us see alternative views and ways of being.

- Our intense emotions help us identify problems and motivate us to fix them.

- Our hyperactivity makes us outgoing and filled with energy. We keep going where others give up.

Another way of figuring out your strengths is to ask yourself these questions:

- What were my achievements this week? What can I give myself a high five for?
- What are my three biggest achievements over my whole life?
- What would other people say they appreciate about you?
- What are five topics or activities that fascinate you?

SET GOALS THAT MATTER TO YOU

We often get caught up in doing things because we think we should. Society expects it. We get pressure from our family to do what they think is best. If you're struggling with your goals, it could well be that they're not *your* goals. They're things other people told you should be your goals. If it doesn't matter to you, you're not going to care about achieving it.

Consider what you really want from life. Then, you can use that to set achievable goals and figure out how you will get there.

Even when you know what you want to do, ADHD can make goal-setting difficult because of our disorganization and executive dysfunction. Make it easy on yourself by starting with this simple three-step process:

- Write down a goal in your Workbook.
- List all the reasons why you want to achieve that goal, no matter how big or small. How will it make you feel? How will it affect your life?

- Now, write down the first small step you're going to take to get closer to your goal. Then do it – today!

CUT BACK THE OVERWHELM

Goals can be a struggle because they are overwhelming. That's why we've talked about breaking things down into smaller, actionable steps. You might not be able to take over the world as a best-selling author today, but you could write 500 words of your novel. When you've completed those 500 words, celebrate your achievement. Treat yourself to a coffee from your favorite coffee shop. Go see a movie. Tell a supportive friend that you've hit today's target, and let them celebrate you.

You might find it helpful to start by deciding the smallest amount of time you want to devote to your goal right now. Even if you only do five minutes, you've made progress, and those five minutes can lead to ten, twenty, an hour. Then, tell yourself that if you spend that time working on your goal, you get to enjoy the rest of your day, feeling great because you've done something on your goals.

You don't have to do everything right now. You just have to do something. Find the smallest thing you can do towards your goal and start there. And remember that if you're putting off a task because you simply don't want to do it, you can always outsource it.

MOTIVATE YOURSELF

Our brain's neurochemistry can make it difficult to get motivated, thanks to our lack of dopamine. You can take steps to overcome this by finding ways to motivate yourself.

- If you find yourself procrastinating, review Chapter 15. Remember why your goal is important, and use the strategies outlined to work towards it.

- Think of times when you successfully completed a similar task to remind yourself that you can do it.

- Know that it's okay not to feel amazing about doing something. Tell yourself, "I can do this. If I want to reach my goals, I have to be the one to get there."

- Be kind to yourself. Don't try and bootstrap your way through. Instead, congratulate yourself on your efforts without worrying about whether it's good enough. You're doing your best, and the more you work on things, the more you'll improve.

You might find it helpful to give yourself a pep talk to boost your morale. You'll find space in your Workbook to draft what you might say to yourself when you're feeling unmotivated. Then, look at yourself in the mirror while you recite your speech. It might feel strange at first, but I promise it really does work! Include phrases like:

- Every little step I take gets me closer to my goals.

- I have good reasons for wanting to achieve my goals.

- When I procrastinate, I make it harder to reach my goals. I will do something towards my goals every day, even if I don't feel like it.

- I will feel amazing when I've achieved my goal.

MANAGE YOUR MOOD

Review Chapter 20 to regulate your emotions and help you overcome emotional hurdles while working toward your goals. Before you start work on your goal, take a few minutes to check in with your emotions and consider how you can ask for help if needed. Build your emotional vocabulary by describing your feelings in as much detail as possible.

There's an exercise in your Workbook to give you a chance to practice understanding and articulating how you feel. Taking time to understand how you're feeling will not only help you become more self-aware, but it will also support the work you've been doing on emotional regulation. It will help you get in the mood to stay on track with your goals and find the confidence to work through emotional barriers that come up, like frustration, anger, or other emotions that might stand in your way.

If you're getting frustrated with your progress, take a step back. Could you ask for help? Rather than banging your head against a wall, recognize when you can't do it alone. You may find resources online that will help, or you may know someone who can solve your problem. Use what you learned in the Workbook exercise to help you get what you need.

TAKE A HEALTHY APPROACH

We've gone over the importance of good habits throughout this book. This is one example of why it's so important to make healthy lifestyle choices. Even when you're not actively working on your goals, you could be undermining your efforts if you're not supporting your health. It's much harder to focus and pay attention when you're hungry or sleep-deprived.

Remember to:

- Practice good sleep habits.
- Manage your stress with the strategies in this book.
- Get regular exercise.
- Take naps and regular breaks. Don't try to push through if you're starting to get distracted and struggling to concentrate.

Follow the six guidelines shown in the sections above, and you'll find it's much easier to reach your goals.

Goals can cover all aspects of your life, but a lot of our goals tend to focus on success in the workplace. That's why I've devoted the final section of this book entirely to how to build a thriving professional life.

PART 5

Professional Life, Superhuman Skills & The Importance of Support

22

YOUR QUIRKS AT WORK ARE YOUR TRADEMARK

Standing Out In A Sea Of Sameness

"Finish each day and be done with it. You have done what you could. Some blunders and absurdities no doubt crept in, forget them as soon as you can. Tomorrow is a new day."

– Ralph Waldo Emerson

> *Before I had children, I worked in admin and I hated it. I lived in constant fear I would be fired because I was so disorganized. After I had my daughter, I decided I wanted to find a job I could do from home and work around her needs. I ended up training as a hairdresser and I love it! I have a room in my house set aside as my salon and I also do home visits. I never spend more than an hour with each client and they're all so different. I love hearing about what's new in their lives. It doesn't seem to matter how long I work. It only ever feels like five minutes. – Melissa G.*

There is a very simple trick to building a career when you have ADHD: do a job that works with your strengths. Some roles are almost impossible for our ADHD brains. I came to terms a long time ago with the fact that I'd never be a surgeon or an accountant. I just don't have the focus or the dedication. But when I sat down, thought about my strengths (as suggested in Chapter 21), and looked at what careers I might be good at, I was surprised at how many options I had.

Stop worrying about what you can't do and focus on what you can. If you're struggling to succeed in your current role, it could be you're trying to force your uniquely shaped self into an ill-fitting hole. You might need a fast-paced job for your fast brain where there isn't too much structure and the hours are flexible. Or you may be better suited to entrepreneurship, where you have control of your environment and hours.

These are just some of the careers that may appeal to ADHD minds. These are not to be seen as a list of recommendations. Rather, you might view this as an interesting way of identifying what triggers your interests. Do any of these provoke a feeling of excitement? Do they help you to see a clear difference between what you currently do and what would feel great to do? If so, perhaps this is the start of a new direction for you … ?

- Teaching or working with children
- Journalist
- Editor
- Chef
- Beautician
- Hair stylist
- Entrepreneur or small business owner
- Nurse
- High-tech industries such as IT or software development
- Artist
- Stage manager
- Firefighter
- Massage Therapist
- Advertising Creative Director
- Wildlife Biologist
- Flight Attendant
- Video Game Designer
- Occupational Therapist
- Stylist
- Public Relations Specialist
- Interior Designer
- Park Ranger
- Radio DJ
- Dental Hygienist
- Athletic Coach

- Librarian
- Real Estate Agent
- Psychologist
- Landscape Architect
- Musician
- Nutritionist
- Nonprofit Program Coordinator
- Zoologist
- Freelance Consultant
- Crime Scene Investigator
- Yoga Instructor
- Archaeologist
- Air Traffic Controller
- Animator
- Special Education Teacher
- Outdoor Adventure Guide

Trust me. Life gets so much easier when you're doing a job you love rather than pushing through your problems to maintain an unsuitable role, only to burn yourself out.

REASONABLE ACCOMMODATIONS FOR ADHD

Even if you're in a job you love, you may well benefit from your workplace making some adjustments to support you. ADHD is a recognized disability under the law, and you could be entitled to accommodations including:

- Job restructuring.
- Working from home.
- Part-time or shared roles.

- Flexible working hours.

- Specific equipment, devices, and training, such as getting a sit-stand desk. These are adjustable desks you can move while you're working, making it easier for you to fidget while you focus. If you need to use headsets for your job, consider getting wireless ones so you can move around while you're on a call.

- ADHD-friendly company policies. These might include having clear written instructions for completing tasks or projects, providing ADHD training for all employees, including management, so they understand more about its impact, or recording meetings so everyone has a record of what was discussed and agreed.

- Private or quiet places to work. This means no doors opening and closing, no noisy machinery, and no distracting phone calls.

- Noise-canceling headphones or white noise playing.

- Bringing in an ADHD coach. Coaching usually lasts between 3-6 months so you can learn skills you need to do your job effectively in a way that works with your ADHD.

Under the Americans with Disabilities Act (ADA), you qualify for accommodations if you can perform the essential functions of your role with them. The important thing is that you are capable of fulfilling all required duties, with or without accommodations.

When applying for a job, read the description carefully. If there are areas where you feel you would need accommodations, it is worth discussing them during the interview. If you are already employed and feel that accommodations would make you more efficient and effective, go back to your job description and identify the parts where accommodations would help. Not everyone needs accommodations. It is up to you to determine whether you would benefit. You may find that the strategies laid out in this book are all you need to do your best.

HOW TO ASK FOR ACCOMMODATIONS

It can be intimidating to ask for accommodations. As women, we can be bad at advocating for ourselves because we tend to put the needs of others before our own. We may also feel – rightly or wrongly – that we'll be viewed as demanding. However, if you have a diagnosis and the documentation to support it, you are completely within your rights to ask.

You can prepare yourself for asking for accommodations by:

- Detailing how ADHD affects you and your work so you have a written list to refer to.

- Printing out your job description and highlighting every duty you need support with. Add reasons for why accommodation is necessary.

- Give examples of appropriate accommodations that will help you.

- Explain how your accommodations will help the company. Some employers are more understanding when they can see how everyone benefits when you're a more productive, effective employee.

You'll find space in your Workbook for working through this process.

Once you've fully prepared to approach your manager, request a private meeting to discuss accommodations with them. Be prepared to negotiate. They may have different ideas about what would be reasonable, and their ideas may even be better than yours. If in doubt, refer back to your notes and stay true to your needs.

BE YOUR OWN ADVOCATE

You don't have to power through your problems alone, but if you don't speak up for yourself, others may not notice you're struggling. Get comfortable with negotiating with your co-workers for help with things you find tough. Try to approach people who excel where you struggle and offer to do things they find challenging in return.

In Chapter 21, you identified your strengths. Now, it's time to do the same with your weaknesses. When, where, and how do they cause you problems?

Remember that your ADHD does not define you. It may cause you challenges, but you can overcome them with the right approach and help. Be aware of when your ADHD makes things more difficult. When you're under stress or pressured to meet a deadline, you may find your ADHD symptoms are worse. Some environments can be harder to work in, say, if they're noise and distraction-filled or you're confined to a desk. These are all things that can be discussed to see what accommodations can be made.

Come back to your strengths list when you're feeling disheartened. The more you can bring your strengths to your daily life, the better you'll feel about yourself. Educate others about what works for you and speak up to adapt environments to be more ADHD-friendly. You may find that even neurotypical people enjoy an environment adapted for ADHD women too.

One final point: don't wait to "get over" ADHD before you give yourself permission to follow your dreams. ADHD will always be an important part of you. Lean into your strengths to remain true to your authentic self. Accept who you are and let your natural talents guide your decisions. You'll find life becomes far less of a struggle when you shine the spotlight on your strengths instead of trying to improve the weaknesses that are an integral part of your brain's mechanics.

Life doesn't have to be a struggle. There's nothing more wonderful than an ADHD brain all excited about doing something it loves. Things *can* be easy – but you have to be prepared to do the work to make things easy.

If you still think you'll find it hard to advocate for yourself, I've got you covered. In the next chapter, we'll examine communication skills so you can feel confident in speaking up.

23

LEADING WITH EMPATHY

Your ADHD Advantage In Communication

"Women speaking up for themselves and for those around them is the strongest force we have to change the world."

– Melinda Gates

My smart mouth always got me into trouble. I would say the wrong thing. People would take offense at something I thought was funny. Once my reputation as a troublemaker was established, it became harder for people to believe me when I said I needed help. They thought I was just messing around again.

It's only since my diagnosis that people have started to take me seriously. Fortunately, being known as a troublemaker makes it easier for me to speak up when I see something wrong. It's not as easy for other people, so here are a few ways you can get comfortable with being your own advocate. In your Workbook you'll find the space and freedom to jot down and explore any thoughts you may have about self-advocacy and communication. Keep it in mind as you continue, and be sure to use it!

WHAT IS SELF-ADVOCACY?

Self-advocacy is:

- Being able to speak up for yourself
- Being confident in making your own decisions
- Knowing how to get the necessary information
- Learning who is able to support you
- Understanding your rights and responsibilities
- Problem-solving
- Knowing when to ask for help
- Listening to and learning from others

Self-advocacy enables you to take more control over your life and get what you need to be your best self. Sadly, for many women, it is hard to speak up because we don't want to be viewed as bossy or demanding. ADHD can also make the idea of self-advocacy anxiety-inducing.

Try to focus on the benefits. When you self-advocate, the rewards can be seen in improved working conditions. ADHD is still broadly misunderstood, so when you educate others about your condition and ask for what you need to be successful, not only do you improve your life, but you also potentially help others improve theirs.

THE THREE STEPS TO SELF-ADVOCACY

Self-advocacy is easier than it may have seemed. There are three main aspects:

- Know what you need
- Know what support is possible
- Communicate your needs clearly

That's it! Self-advocacy is so important in the workplace. It leads to open communication where co-workers understand each other better, improving conditions for all. This helps avoid toxic relationships with co-workers, leading to healthier connections.

When you advocate for your needs, you'll feel that your worth is recognized and appreciated, helping you avoid burnout. Getting the support and resources you need to do your job fosters an environment of fairness and respect. You'll feel more secure in your job and demonstrate that you are committed to building a healthy, productive workplace.

Self-advocacy can also help grow your career prospects. Many people who feel there's no room for development in their current position leave for opportunities elsewhere. You could be leaving a dream job with lots of potential for no good reason when if you'd only talked about your concerns with your boss, you might have found a solution together. You may discover that you're much better at your job than you thought you were once reasonable adjustments have been made. You could end up being a star member of your team because of all your ADHD superpowers!

When you have the confidence to speak up when things feel stagnant, you give your employer the chance to support your career and unveil new opportunities. You might like to review the list of possible workplace accommodations in Chapter 22 for suggestions about what can be done to make you more effective at work.

If you can't advocate for yourself, then do it for others. As we've already seen, when you advocate for yourself, everyone benefits. When accommodations are put in place for one person, it helps others create a work environment conducive to peak performance. Not only are you showing you're a valuable team player, but leading by example will give others the courage to speak up, too.

If you still think self-advocacy seems intimidating, have no fear. It's a skill you can learn, just like all the others we've covered. Here are seven ways you can be better at self-advocacy. You'll recognize some of them, which will help you see that self-advocacy is nothing to fear.

KNOW YOUR STRENGTHS AND WEAKNESSES

In the previous two chapters, we identified your strengths and weaknesses. You should now know where you need help most.

Can you achieve your targets with what you already have? If not, what do you need to get the job done?

KNOW YOUR RIGHTS

How can you stand up for your rights if you don't know what they are?

Research your rights and responsibilities in the workplace. A meeting with HR may be helpful if you can't find the information online. You may not know what you're entitled to under the law, but your employer is legally obliged to provide you with fair pay and a safe workplace. Likewise, you need to know what you need to do in terms of your performance and your job requirements so you can make sure you're upholding your end of the agreement.

ASK FOR HELP

Sometimes, you can't do everything yourself. Knowing when to ask for help is a sign of strength, not weakness. It shows self-awareness and a commitment to getting things done. It also demonstrates courage by being vulnerable. If you've been working through the various exercises in this book and in your Workbook, you should have a better understanding of where you need help and what would be most useful.

UNDERSTAND YOUR VALUE

What do you bring to the table? What does that mean for the business?

Your skills, personality, and experience combine to make you a valuable team member. Your ADHD can give you all sorts of benefits, such as creativity (whether that be designing or making something or problem-solving), the willingness to take risks, the ability to think outside the box, hyperfocus, staying calm in a crisis, and being detail-oriented. All of these are helpful in a work environment.

Even where you perceive some skill gaps, these are opportunities for growth rather than failures to beat yourself up about. You're building on the strong foundation of who you are already. Your workplace may be able to help you with training to help plug those gaps.

BE OPEN AND RESPECTFUL IN YOUR COMMUNICATIONS

Don't expect your co-workers to be mind readers. You advocate most effectively when you're direct in your requests. This doesn't mean being aggressive, which is counterproductive. But make it clear what you're asking for and why. Then, listen to the reply and any needs your co-workers may be communicating. You may need to negotiate to get what you want, so be open to finding some common ground and a solution that works for everyone. Review the advice given in Chapter Ten about interpersonal effectiveness, particularly the DEARMAN skill, for ways of communicating with your co-workers.

BE PROUD OF YOUR ACHIEVEMENTS

Women can be shy about telling others what they've achieved. We don't want to be seen as show-offs. But it's important to make people aware of the things you've done. If you've won an award, don't be afraid to display it on your desk. When you have an appraisal, tell your manager about all your recent achievements.

Sometimes, people need a helping hand to notice how awesome you are. There's nothing wrong with making your value clear.

BE ASSERTIVE

Assertiveness is the confidence to express yourself, set and maintain boundaries, and consider others' rights and needs.

One way to be assertive is to set yourself goals that are specific, measurable, and achievable. This could mean negotiating a pay rise or arranging a meeting with your boss to discuss accommodations. When you know exactly what you want to achieve, you know it's possible and you decide when you need it by, it makes it easier to find the confidence to advocate for yourself. This can also involve asking for training to develop skills that will help you – even assertiveness training!

Ultimately, self-advocacy doesn't mean you're putting yourself above someone else. You're simply asserting yourself and your needs while respecting others and their needs. It's finding the middle ground between standing up for yourself without riding roughshod over others.

One way of helping you find the confidence to advocate for yourself is to celebrate your personal success. I think it's so important that I've devoted an entire chapter to it, coming up next.

24

FINDING YOUR PROFESSIONAL NICHE
Aligning Career With ADHD Strengths

"The very traits that once held Ty back are now his greatest assets."

– Yvonne Pennington, mother of Ty Pennington

When you've grown up like I have, losing things, forgetting appointments, mixing up your schedule, you quickly learn how to be flexible. While I still have my days when I wish I didn't have ADHD because of all the problems it's caused me, I take time out to think about all the gifts I have because of it, too.

That flexibility means I think fast. I find solutions quicker than anyone I know. I know how to compensate when things don't go as planned. Sometimes, they've gone wrong because of something I've done, but I don't beat myself up for it anymore. I laugh and see it as another opportunity to practice my super-powerful, creative problem-solving skills.

Everyone has strengths and weaknesses, even if they don't have ADHD. Nobody's perfect. Accepting and embracing your unique ADHD personality will help your self-esteem immensely.

FIND YOUR PEOPLE

We'll look at building your support squad in more depth in the next chapter, but I wanted to mention now the importance of speaking up for others. In the previous chapter, we looked at self-advocacy. It can have a powerful ripple effect. When you speak up to request reasonable adjustments, you pave the way for others to get their needs met, too. In taking a stand for your ADHD needs, you could, in small but important ways, be changing the world!

You'll find that people with ADHD naturally gravitate towards each other. We seem to instinctively recognize people on the same wavelength as us. As more and more of my friends have found the courage to seek their own neurodiverse diagnoses, it's become a running joke that if you're my friend, you've got a 99% chance of being neurodiverse in one form or another!

We all support each other, pointing out our strengths when we're having a bad day. Because I know that I'm bad at staying in touch, even though I really want to, I don't mind when my friends are just as bad. I know it doesn't mean we don't care. We have the best times when we do see each other. I don't think I laugh as much as I do when I'm with my closest ADHD friends.

SET UP EDUCATION AND TRAINING SESSIONS

As the resident expert for ADHD in your company, you could take the lead on setting up education and training sessions for your co-workers. You could ask friends with ADHD or known experts to come in and talk about their experience with ADHD, how it affects people, and what everyone can do to be more inclusive and supportive of ADHD.

Education is one of the most powerful ways of reducing the stigma surrounding ADHD and increasing empathy and understanding of those living with the condition.

PROMOTE OPEN CONVERSATIONS

Encourage your co-workers to talk about their experience with ADHD. It may be that they suspect they have it themselves or have been recently diagnosed. They could have a family member with the disorder. You could ask people to submit their ADHD stories and create a leaflet to share with your co-workers filled with stories of what it's really like and celebrate any successes.

This is a good way of combating stigma and creating an inclusive workplace culture where more employees can find the courage to be their authentic selves.

SET UP AN ADHD EMPLOYEE RESOURCE GROUP (ERGS)

Companies like IBM, Walgreens, and Bank of America all have ADHD ERGs. Why don't you get your company to join them? ERGs give an opportunity for those with ADHD or affected by it to connect and support each other. It's a useful resource, providing people with the means to network, share information, and advocate for better accommodations in the workplace.

SET UP FUNDRAISING EVENTS AND AWARENESS CAMPAIGNS

ADHD Awareness Month is the perfect chance to arrange events promoting ADHD awareness, such as fundraisers like charity walks, webinars, or workshops. Donate any proceeds raised to an organization supporting ADHD. Not only does this give you an opportunity to celebrate the amazing people in your company who have ADHD, but you're also helping improve the general understanding of ADHD and furthering research into ADHD. (As an added bonus for your company, it may be tax deductible.)

There is so much to be gained by recognizing and celebrating the impact ADHD has on your life. Setting up events to promote awareness doesn't just help others with ADHD; it also helps you recognize your important contribution to the world. Using your unique voice and experiences to promote understanding is a powerful way to foster change and understanding for the good of all. I've created space in your Workbook where you can brainstorm how you'd like to celebrate ADHD. Use the space as you please. Perhaps you could use it to plan an event!

It might seem like a big commitment to get involved in community advocacy, but there's nothing to say you have to do it alone. In the next and last chapter, we'll look at how you can build your support team to lift each other to even greater heights.

25

YOUR ADHD TRIBE

Creating A Network
That Elevates You

"People with ADHD have a hard time making friends. We have so much to offer in friendship. We are creative, fun, quirky, and empathetic."

– Caroline Maguire

Looking back, growing up, I was a textbook example of a girl with ADHD. But if you think women with ADHD are misunderstood now, we've come on leaps and bounds since I was a child. ADHD was apparently something that only affected boys. Being a girl, the fault had to be with me. I was lazy. Overly talkative. Easily distracted.

I graduated high school thinking I was stupid and would never amount to anything. I certainly never believed I could have written a book, yet here you are, holding it!

I'm far from alone in my story. Studies suggest that as many as 75% of girls with ADHD are undiagnosed, leaving us to struggle through by ourselves[1]. We're left to cope with our feelings of inadequacy and failure without any support. Our self-esteem plummets. We convince ourselves that we're worthless.

You shouldn't have to deal with this alone. Thankfully, you don't! You are among millions of women living with ADHD. There's a community of us ready and waiting to welcome you with open arms.

FINDING FRIENDS ONLINE

The internet has opened up a world of resources, so even if you don't feel ready to seek out real-life friendships, you'll find plenty of groups filled with supportive women who just want to help their fellow sisters. Simply search for ADHD in women on your favorite social media platform, and you'll be given countless groups to choose from. Online groups work really well if you don't have much spare time. You can check in at a time that suits you and participate at whatever level you prefer.

Some groups are women only, and others are not. It's up to you where you feel most comfortable sharing your experiences. Read the group description before joining to see whether it aligns with your values. Once you've joined, you might like to read without posting for a few days to get a feel for a group and see whether you feel comfortable there. You may even find that you offer help to others before you ask for it yourself.

Maybe start with the LearnWell Community?

I have never met some of my closest friends in real life. We've known each other for years online, and despite never having gotten together in person, I've never encountered such generous people. One time when I was feeling particularly down, one of my online friends sent me an essential oil blend designed especially to lift my mood. When I was having problems at work, my online friends were the ones who offered me suggestions on how to talk about it with my boss and cheered me on when I told them how everything was solved – with their help, of course.

FINDING LOCAL SUPPORT GROUPS

While I'm a big fan of online support groups, nothing beats personal interaction. Meeting up with other women with ADHD beats the loneliness that can come with the condition. They'll have solutions for the problems you're facing because they've been through it themselves. They'll show you the light at the end of the tunnel.

You can find details of support groups in your area through organizations such as CHADD and the Attention Deficit Disorder

Association, which hold networking and educational events. If you can't find a group that suits you, don't hesitate to start your own. It's easy to do. Spread the word by putting up posters at the library, in church, and in local stores. Contact local ADHD organizations and clinicians to see if they'll help you find members.

While you don't need your group organized by a professional, you will need someone to handle the administrative side of things, such as arranging meetings and any extras like finding speakers. If you know that you will struggle to keep up with this, don't be afraid to ask around for someone to help you.

Be specific about what you want from your group. A support group for women with ADHD will have a different feel and set up to one, for example, for couples affected by ADHD.

BEING A POSITIVE MEMBER OF A GROUP

Whether you're part of an online or in-person support group, there are a few things you can do to make the most of your membership.

- Save talking for the appropriate moment. Much as it can be hard to control our outbursts – and an ADHD group should understand that more than most! – try to keep chatter for the right time. Some support groups incorporate socializing as part of the group structure, while others offer scheduled chances to make friends before and/or after the organized meeting.

- Observe the group dynamic before sharing about yourself. Saying too much about yourself can make others feel uncomfortable but if you clam up, people might think you're standoffish. The right group will feel like you've come home, and you'll feel welcome to be your true self. If you don't, it's okay to find a different group.

- Support others. As a good rule of thumb, try to make three replies to other peoples' comments for every time you talk about yourself. The more you give, the more you'll get out of a group.

There's a world of neurodiverse women out there waiting to be your friend. Once you start building those connections, you'll discover there's no feeling like knowing that you're part of a community that accepts you just as you are. In your Workbook, there are a few blank journal pages for you to use as you like. If there are any specific points you'd like to remember from this chapter or any ideas that might have popped up for you, use that space to explore them.

IN 90 SECONDS YOU CAN MAKE A HUGE DIFFERENCE

If you feel we've deserved it, please take a moment to leave a review on Amazon.

Your feedback means the world to us. It helps us to improve and it means better learning experiences for all our readers.

We'd be so grateful to you for your review!

CONCLUSION

No one can ever truly understand the impact ADHD has on you unless they have it themselves. Getting a diagnosis literally changed my life. It enabled me to understand myself better and let go of those feelings of guilt and shame that had been my constant companion.

I'm not going to pretend that everything's sunshine and roses just because of my diagnosis. I've still had to do plenty of work to overcome the hurdles ADHD puts in my way. The work never stops, either.

The good news is that it gets easier as I've become used to doing certain things. It's second nature for me to make my Daily Checklist now. When I'm in a difficult situation, I turn to the toolbox I've developed, thanks to CBT and DBT. I speak up about my needs in a firm but respectful way. I haven't just learned how to advocate for myself. I'm often the person that friends come to when they need support in advocating for themselves.

The best part is that I see my ADHD for what it is: my superpower. I don't focus on my weaknesses now. I know that I'm bad at staying in touch, even with the help of reminders and notes, so I make sure to compensate when I see my friends by making sure that we have a great time together. As I've discovered more about my strengths, I've been able to see that my ADHD has made me who I am. Without my neurodivergent brain, I wouldn't be the creative soul that I am, overflowing with ideas. I wouldn't have the empathy for others that I do that makes me so understanding and nurturing. I wouldn't have my quirky sense of humor that has my friends laughing until they cry.

I can't help but think how boring I would be if I didn't have ADHD.

I hope that you have found the strategies in this book helpful. Even if you implement only a fraction of what you've learned, I'm sure you'll soon see a change for the better. And maybe, as you see improvements, you'll be inspired to use other suggestions from this book.

Welcome to the world of women with ADHD. We're pretty darned awesome!

REFERENCES

Introduction

1. https://www.healthline.com/health/adhd/facts-statistics-infographic#fast-facts

Chapter One

1. https://www.ncbi.nlm.nih.gov/pmc/articles/PMC10631790/
2. https://psychcentral.com/adhd/adhd-and-gender#diagnosis
3. https://link.springer.com/article/10.1007/s10578-021-01159-w

Chapter Two

1. https://www.ncbi.nlm.nih.gov/pmc/articles/PMC7422602/
2. https://adhdgirlsandwomen.org/wp-content/uploads/2022/05/Hinshaw_2021_Review.pdf
3. https://www.maps-medical.co.uk/insights/womens-pain-routinely-underestimated-and-under-treated
4. https://www.ncbi.nlm.nih.gov/pmc/articles/PMC10173330/
5. https://www.healthline.com/health/adhd/adhd-and-hormonal-changes-in-women#estrogen
6. https://www.additudemag.com/puberty-and-adhd-symptoms-teens/
7. https://www.addept.org/living-with-adult-add-adhd/homones-and-adhd

8. https://www.additudemag.com/puberty-and-adhd-symptoms-teens/
9. https://www.additudemag.com/adhd-menopause-women-research/

Chapter Three

1. https://www.medicalnewstoday.com/articles/adhd-brain-vs-normal-brain#key-differences
2. https://www.verywellmind.com/hyperfocus-and-add-20464#:~:text=Children%20and%20adults%20with%20ADHD,that%20it%20is%20called%20hyperfocus.
3. https://www.healthline.com/health/adhd/iq-adhd
4. https://edition.cnn.com/2018/06/06/health/adhd-medication-adult/index.html
5. https://www.openaccessgovernment.org/four-signs-of-adhd-in-women-different-adhd-men-anxiety-depression-diagnosis/135332/
6. https://www.ncbi.nlm.nih.gov/pmc/articles/PMC4403287/
7. https://www.webmd.com/add-adhd/adult-adhd-facts-statistics

Chapter Four

1. https://www.ncbi.nlm.nih.gov/pmc/articles/PMC9821724/
2. https://www.betterhealth.vic.gov.au/health/healthyliving/breathing-to-reduce-stress#

Chapter Five

1. https://www.ncbi.nlm.nih.gov/pmc/articles/PMC5573739/
2. https://www.addept.org/living-with-adult-add-adhd/why-are-my-feelings-so-intense

Chapter Six

1. https://www.mayoclinichealthsystem.org/hometown-health/speaking-of-health/can-expressing-gratitude-improve-health

Chapter Seven

1. https://en.wikipedia.org/wiki/Nonviolent_Communication

Chapter Eight

1. https://www.psychologytoday.com/intl/blog/living-forward/202009/how-your-thinking-creates-your-reality

Chapter Nine

1. https://www.apa.org/monitor/dec07/adults
2. https://www.verywellmind.com/adhd-and-motivation-20470

Chapter Ten

1. https://ascellus.com/learn-the-broken-record-technique/#:~:text=The%20Broken%20Record%20Technique%20is,with%20treatment%2C%20forgetful%20or%20disorganized.

Chapter Eleven

1. https://trends.google.com/trends/explore?date=all&q=mindfulness&hl=en
2. https://www.sciencedirect.com/science/article/abs/pii/S0148296323006446

Chapter Twelve

1. https://www.verywellmind.com/causes-and-symptoms-of-time-blindness-in-adhd-5216523#:~:text=The%20need%20for%20emotional%20stimulation,in%20ADHD%20to%20dopamine%20deficiencies.
2. https://www.ncbi.nlm.nih.gov/pmc/articles/PMC8293837/

Chapter Thirteen

1. https://www.ncbi.nlm.nih.gov/pmc/articles/PMC7485505/
2. https://www.medicalnewstoday.com/articles/adhd-and-organization#:~:text=People%20with%20ADHD%20may%20have,and%20can%20affect%20organizational%20skills.

Chapter Fourteen

1. https://www.verywellmind.com/adhd-benefits-advantages-challenges-and-tips-5199254#:~:text=It's%20a%20neurotype%2C%20which%20means,can%20wield%20to%20their%20advantage.
2. https://www.verywellmind.com/perfectionism-adhd-symptom-5496248#:~:text=The%20Link%20Between%20ADHD%20and%20Perfectionism&text=Studies%20also%20find%20a%20strong,rash%20decisions%20out%20of%20frustration.
3. https://www.additudemag.com/how-to-plan-ahead-when-you-have-adhd-understand-time/

Chapter Fifteen

1. https://www.aacap.org/AACAP/Families_and_Youth/Facts_for_Families/FFF-Guide/ADHD_and_the_Brain-121.

2. aspx#:~:text=The%20brain%20is%20divided%20 into,pay%20attention%2C%20and%20make%20decisions.
2. https://www.ncbi.nlm.nih.gov/pmc/articles/ PMC2626918/#:~:text=People%20with%20ADHD%20 have%20at,and%20the%20regulation%20of%20attention.
3. https://www.verywellmind.com/anxiety-in-adults-with-adhd-20758#:~:text=Common%20features%20of%20 these%20disorders,%2C%20fatigue%2C%20and%20 feeling%20overwhelmed.
4. https://www.understood.org/en/articles/adhd-and-perfectionism
5. https://www.helpguide.org/articles/add-adhd/adhd-attention-deficit-hyperactivity-disorder-in-women.htm
6. https://www.additudemag.com/adhd-motivation-problems-getting-started-on-tough-projects/
7. https://en.wikipedia.org/wiki/Decision_fatigue

Chapter Sixteen

1. https://www.ncbi.nlm.nih.gov/pmc/articles/ PMC10421702/#:~:text=Increased%20susceptibility%20 to%20internal%20forms,rather%20than%20on%20 internal%20distracting
2. https://en.wikipedia.org/wiki/Object_permanence

Chapter Seventeen

1. https://www.ncbi.nlm.nih.gov/pmc/articles/PMC9322602/
2. https://www.additudemag.com/nutrition-harmonizes-adhd-brain/#:~:text=D.%2C%20and%20others%20have%20 shown,protein%2Drich%20breakfast%20and%20lunch.
3. https://pubmed.ncbi.nlm.nih.gov/34139473/

4. https://www.healthline.com/nutrition/low-glycemic-diet#the-bottom-line
5. https://www.additudemag.com/slideshows/adhd-supplements-fish-oil-zinc-iron/
6. https://www.mindlabpro.com/blogs/nootropics/b6-and-dopamine#:~:text=Vitamin%20B6%20is%20a%20key,dopamine%2C%20noradrenalin%2C%20and%20histamine.&text=B6%20thus%20helps%20increase%20brain,depression%2C%20fatigue%2C%20and%20pain.
7. https://www.additudemag.com/adhd-omega-3-benefits/#:~:text=Better%20memory%2C%20better%20learning.,bed%20%E2%80%94%20with%20omega%2D3s.
8. https://www.mentalhelp.net/adhd/other-therapies/#:~:text=Ginkgo%20and%20Ginseng&text=Ginkgo%20is%20known%20to%20improve,children%20and%20adolescents%20with%20ADHD.
9. https://www.additudemag.com/sugar-diet-nutrition-impact-adhd-symptoms/#:~:text=How%20Does%20Sugar%20Impact%20ADHD,copious%20amounts%20of%20sweet%20stuff.
10. https://www.healthline.com/health/adhd/foods-to-avoid#dyes
11. https://www.everydayhealth.com/adhd-pictures/how-food-can-affect-your-childs-adhd-symptoms.aspx#:~:text=Some%20of%20the%20common%20foods,about%20trying%20an%20elimination%20diet.

Chapter Eighteen

1. https://www.psychologytoday.com/gb/blog/on-your-way-with-adhd/202305/adult-adhd-and-friendship

2. https://www.businessinsider.com/friendship-is-harder-for-people-with-adhd-rejection-masking-2023-10

Chapter Nineteen

1. https://pubmed.ncbi.nlm.nih.gov/29301669/
2. Dodson, W. (2021). Emotional Sensitivity and Intensity in ADHD. ADDitude Magazine.
3. Smith, A., & Anderson, M. (2020). 5 facts about online dating. Pew Research Center.
4. https://journals.sagepub.com/doi/abs/10.1177/0886260515586371?journalCode=jiva

Chapter Twenty

1. https://www.additudemag.com/emotional-dysregulation-adhd-video/#:~:text=%E2%80%9CEmotion%20regulation%20is%20a%20big,part%20of%20the%20prefrontal%20cortex.

Chapter Twenty-Five

1. https://caddac.ca/adhd-in-women-and-girls/